CHRISTMAS GIFTS
Ten of the Greatest Ever Given

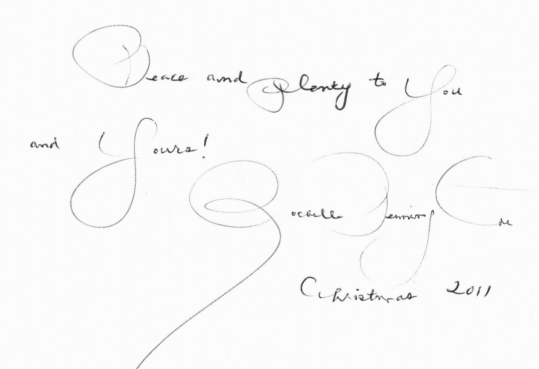

Peace and Plenty to You and Yours!

Christmas 2011

CHRISTMAS GIFTS

Ten of the Greatest Ever Given

ROCHELLE PENNINGTON

Published by Pathways Press
1-800-503-5507

ISBN: 978-0-9740810-6-9

Published by Pathways Press
1-800-503-5507

Manufactured in Canada

DEDICATION

For my husband, Leslie, to whom my heart belongs.

TABLE OF CONTENTS

INTRODUCTION

It is a gift I remember well, a gift given during a difficult Christmas for my family.

My dad had been sick for a long time—too long. He had spent three months in the hospital already, and there were no promises he would make it home for Christmas. The doctor told my mom: "Maybe for a visit, but only for twenty-four hours." Then the coming home would mean the going back, but we remained thankful for anything we were able to hope for that year, even if it wasn't much.

That said, mom ordered a hospital bed and set it up in the living room next to the tree—just in case. Then all five of us kids took turns sleeping in it while we waited for dad to come home.

Lots of folks heard about my father living at the hospital and felt bad like we did. I remember many of those people showing up at our door to give my mom cookies, a fruit basket, a kettle of soup, a loaf of bread, or a casserole.

Even strangers came. One nameless woman knocked on our door one evening and said to my mom when she answered, "You don't know me, but I work with your sister over at the Amity factory. She told me about your husband, and I just wanted to do something to help."

Then she started crying, and my mom started crying, and I thought, "Gosh, what is going on? Why is everyone crying? Didn't this lady just say that she didn't even know my mom?"

I was stumped. The nameless woman I never saw before, and would never see again, was crying in my mother's arms like I would have. It really made me think. It was a Christmas, in all truth, where a lot of things made me think—like what Mr. Skretny at the corner drug store did.

He spotted me standing in one of his aisles in front of bottles of men's cologne.

"Something for your dad?" he asked. "I heard he's coming home."

Yes, dad was coming home, and, yes, I needed a present, but, no, I was not going to be able to afford anything on those shelves. (That much I had figured out as I stared at the prices on Old Spice, dad's favorite.)

"Maybe I'll get him some Chapstick," I mumbled, embarrassed that the money stuffed inside my little red mitten, almost all change, wasn't nearly enough for even the smallest bottle of any brand.

"Oh, your dad doesn't like cologne?" asked Mr. Skretny as he walked toward me, knowing more of what was going on in my little mind than I could have realized.

I didn't want to answer Mr. Skretny's question, so I didn't. I just wanted to get out of there, and I would have done just that had he not come over to stand beside me where, together, we looked at the bottles lined up neatly. Old Spice, Old Spice, Old Spice.

"How much do you have to spend?" asked the man who smelled like dad.

"Not enough," I told him. It was a simple, matter-of-fact, right-to-the-point kind of answer that let him know that I was not only short, I was *way* short, which he probably knew already.

Then, a miracle. Mr. Skretny reached up and grabbed hold of a top-shelf item above the individual bottles and handed it to me. The ultimate gathering of Old Spice products was inside the box: cologne, aftershave, and soap-on-a-rope. *Wow! Dare I breathe? How could I afford such a present?*

The answer was that I couldn't. Mr. Skretny knew this when he brought the box down and placed it in my hands.

"Wrap this for your father and tell him it's from you," he said, "and have yourself a nice Christmas."

I headed back home that afternoon with my mitten full of money, carrying a gift that was so much better than Chapstick.

"To: Daddy, From: Rochelle"—those were the words written on a tag attached to one of the best presents I have ever given.

Dad loved it, I knew he would, but I loved it more because of Mr. Skretny's generosity to me that afternoon down at the corner drug store. It was so unexpected, so thoughtful, and so needed that year when my family was struggling.

Dad and I both received a Christmas present from Mr. Skretny—mine just wasn't wrapped.

More than four decades have passed since I sat on the end of a hospital bed in a living room watching my father unwrap his gift, but the impression abides with me still.

In the spirit of Mr. Skretny's kindness from long ago, I offer ten of history's most memorable gifts in the stories that follow. May their lessons bring peace to you and yours this Christmas and always.

WORLD WAR I
CHRISTMAS MIRACLE

War was raging in 1914 along the Western Front in Europe and the rapid conclusion to the conflict which had been anticipated failed to happen. Instead of the battle ending by Christmas, as many believed it would, it widened.

Soldiers, entrenched in narrow, four-foot-wide ditches stretching for hundreds of miles from the North Sea to the Swiss border, stared at a world bare and blasted.

Against this backdrop, Christmas came, and with it, the gift of peace.

Enemy combatants crawled out of their trenches, met in the middle, and impulsively halted a war. A century later, this "grand human moment" is recognized as "the most extraordinary event in military history."

Soldiers unwrapped parcels received from loved ones back home and shared the contents within with their adversaries. They swapped cakes, liquors, plum puddings, and sausages as they celebrated a "silent night," a "holy night," together.

Gunfire ceased, and voices were raised in song. Everything from "Oh, Come All Ye Faithful" to "This is the Day the Lord Hath Made" could be heard in the December darkness as peace prevailed.

Eye-witness accounts survive in diaries, memoirs, archival newspapers, letters, and official war journals.

"Whatever the spirit of Christmas had been before that hour," wrote Stephen Wunderli, "it was now, above all, the spirit of hope, of peace. And for a brief moment, the sound of peace was a carol every soul knew by heart."

"One starry night, nearly a hundred years ago, a lonely soldier thought of home, of Christmas, and sang a carol from his trench in a field. His buddies heard him, and they joined in. Across that field, enemies added their voices to the chorus. And all these years later we still have a chance to listen and to join in."

John McCutcheon

Two newspapers, *The Scotsman* in Edinburgh and the *Daily Sketch* in London, published early articles detailing the World War One Christmas truce shortly after it occurred. Their accounts were based on eye-witness testimony given by Major Buchanan-Dunlop, a serving soldier, as included in a letter he wrote home.

An Edinburgh minister, Reverend G. N. Price, then carried Buchanan-Dulop's letter into his pulpit at St. Paul's Episcopal Church and addressed his parishioners as follows: "During the past few days you may have read in your papers, or in letters that have actually

Daily Sketch newspaper, January 6, 1915

come from the trenches, as I have, of the marvel of the Christmas just past—how in many parts of the firing line there was, by mutual consent, a truce of God; how friend and foe met to exchange some small luxury; how they sang to one another the old Christmas carols and hymns. Is it merely fanciful to say that, on the anniversary of the birth of God's Son, there must have been some gracious influence of the spirit of Christ brooding over the combatants and suggesting, though but for a brief moment, the brotherhood of man in the great family of the Father?"

The pastor's heart was full of wonder at the outpouring of goodwill exchanged in No Man's Land, a battlefield strip of ground in between opposing trenches, and he was not alone.

Since the outbreak of "The Great War," the lines along the Western Front were a place of hell, not heaven. Rival armies endured unimaginable hardships as they tried to survive in earthen-walled trenches dug five to eight feet deep in the middle of barren turnip fields and cabbage patches, now planted with bodies and crosses, row upon row.

During the months of October and November 1914, unending rains fell, flooding the trenches. A continuous baling of water was necessitated, and soldiers, thoroughly saturated, sloshing around, confronted inescapable, oozing mud.

"I used to think I knew what mud was before I came out here, but I was quite mistaken," wrote Arthur Pelham-Burn, a 2nd Lieutenant in the Gordon Highlanders. "The mud here varies from six inches to three and four feet deep, even five feet."

Muck and filth. Both were battled by the sufferers, as surely as bullets and bombs, during those terrible days of trial. Fatigued soldiers ached for home. Who wouldn't?

Their homesickness was companioned by actual sickness in their less-than-sanitary conditions. Of the sixty-five million persons who were ultimately engaged in the war, millions lost their lives from disease in the infested trenches, "graves for the living," rather than from enemy fire.

How then, in such a place, could something so utterly beautiful occur? It is a question easier to ask than it is to answer.

"Peace appeared from somewhere, I know not where," wrote Ernie Williams of the Cheshires. His sentiments were echoed by a private who was quoted in *The Whitehaven News*: "'Peace on earth, goodwill toward men!' It is hardly to be believed, but nevertheless it is quite true that such was the case this Christmas. Who can realize it? It will astound everyone who hears about it, which everyone will do in good time."

Piers Brendon believed the scene he looked upon on that noble night was simply "the most extraordinary celebration of Christmas since those notable goings-on in Bethlehem."

In some places the truce commenced when soldiers heard "Silent Night" sung in German. In other places, it was the song "Home Sweet Home" which reduced those there to tears.

"The Germans sang," remembered Jozef van Ryckeghem, a Belgian chaplain, "in voices at first wavering, then firmer, swelling to a mighty Christmas carol."

Albert Moren, serving in the 2nd Queen's Regiment, recalled a "beautiful moonlit night. Frost was on the ground, white was almost everywhere, and there was a lot of commotion in the German trenches. There were these lights (tiny Christmas trees lit with candles). They sang 'Silent Night'—'Stille Nacht.' I shall never forget it. It was one of the highlights of my life."

The Germans shouted: "No shoot tonight! Sing tonight! Sing tonight!"

Lieutenant Sir Edward Hulse wrote home: "The Germans followed with ballads which both sides knew, singing everything from 'Good

The Daily Mirror newspaper, January 8, 1915

King Wenceslas' to 'Auld Lang Syne,' which we all—English, Scots, Irish, Prussians, Wurttembergers—knew. Everyone joined in. It was absolutely astounding."

"Every dugout had its Christmas tree," remembered Kronprinz Wilhelm, Commander of Germany's 5th Army, "and from all directions came the sound of rough men's voices singing our exquisite old Christmas songs."

No longer were ears assaulted by bombs exploding, nor by moans from a just-wounded soldier. Rather, it was the sound of voices lifted in unison which ultimately ushered in peace, a peace that could be seen with the eyes and heard with the heart.

Puzzled adversaries strained to hear "the burst of song floating on the frosty air," recalled 2nd Lieutenant Charles Bruce Bairnsfather. Soon, in response, soldiers joined the repeated refrains midsong. The mixture of melodies, known since childhood, summoned their thoughts homeward. Tensions eased. Who could fight with a song?

Lance-Corporal Henderson of the Royal Engineers penned a letter to his family which was later reprinted in *The Hampshire Chronicle* newspaper. It read: "We discovered a board stuck up in the German trench. We had our glasses on in a minute. The words were printed in big block letters: 'CONCERT OVER HERE TONIGHT. ALL BRITISH TROOPS WELCOME.'"

Other signs were hoisted up: "MERRY CHRISTMAS," "THANK YOU," and "YOU NO SHOOT, WE NO SHOOT."

"Scottish soldiers started playing the bagpipes," recalled Sergeant-Major Frank Naden of the 6th Cheshires. Bugles were produced and "an orchestra" of horns and harmonicas, along with violins, accordions, and concertinas. Some men whistled and others hummed during those rare moments, "so unpredictable and extraordinary," when peace invaded a war.

"I was gazing toward the German lines and thinking to myself what a different sort of Christmas Eve this was from any I had experienced in the past," wrote Graham Williams, "when suddenly lights began to appear along the top of the German trenches. These were Christmas trees adorned with lit candles, burning steadily. Other guards had, of course, seen the same thing, and quickly awoke those asleep in the shelters, to 'come and see this thing which had come to pass.' Then suddenly our opponents began to sing 'Stille Nacht, Heilige Nacht.' They finished their carol and then we sang 'The First Noel.' When we finished, they all began clapping. And so it went on. First the Germans would sing one of their carols, and then we would sing one of ours, until we started up with 'Oh, Come All Ye Faithful,' and the Germans immediately joined in singing the same hymn to the Latin words 'Adeste Fideles.' And I thought, well, well, this is really a most extraordinary thing—two nations both singing the same carol in the middle of a war. And for an instant, the God of goodwill was once more master of this corner of the earth."

The story of the World War I Christmas miracle is best told through the words of those who were there, those who stood side by side in kinship with foes who became friends, even if only momentarily. Their words illuminate the benevolent gestures and give testimony to one of history's most unforgettable events which unfolded on the blessed eve.

"The stars were shining superbly on the horizon, and soldiers were singing," wrote Robert de Wilde, a captain in the Belgian artillery. "It was unreal, sublime. They were singing: 'Minuit, Chretiens, c'est l'heure solennelle,' 'Adeste Fideles,' 'Les Anges de not Campagnes,' all the songs we used to sing when we were little. The Christmases of long ago were coming to life again, all the things we had known in our childhood—the family, the countryside, the fireside, our eyes dazzled by the tree with its sparkling candles—all the things we now relive in our children."

Photographs taken during the Christmas truce

"Minuit Chretiens (O, Holy Night)," spoken of in the above journal entry, was sung at midnight as church bells, calling worshippers to midnight mass, were rung in distant villages and heard across battlefields. A British war correspondent reported: "A voice, clear and beautiful, was singing the beloved Christmas carol 'O, Holy Night.' And who do you think the singer was? Victor Granier of the Paris Opera. The troops forgot to fire while listening to that wonderful tenor voice."

The emotionally stirring rendition of that sacred song, sung acapella, left soldiers from all sides of the conflict in amazement, "swaying like rocking horses," as they listened to this opera vocalist, a man who had been taken from the stage and sent to a place where comfort was scarce—or non-existent.

"Everyone lay still, listening in the quiet of the night to that marvelous voice," recorded the Wurttembergers of the 246th Reserve Regiment in their official report. An unanswered question was added to the end of their entry: "Is it, in fact, the victory of God's love over all human conflict?"

Some would answer "yes" to that question, including those who chose to wage peace instead of war on that Christmas long ago.

Had the "Light of the World" shown His presence there in the darkness amid those shining candles while troops shouted greetings to one another?

The regimental history of the 13th London recorded: "It was the first Christmas of the war and the enemy, no less than ourselves, felt very homesick. The Germans gave the first sign. A tired sentry in our battalion, looking out over the waste toward the German lines, spread the exciting news that the enemy's trenches were 'all alight.' He had hardly uttered the words before other sentries took up the cry and we all looked at the enemy's line, which was dotted here and there with clusters of lights. From behind the lines came German

Eye-Witness Testimony
to the Spontaneous Singing

"I am sure you are anxious to know how we spent Christmas, and I will tell you in detail, but first of all I must describe what will, I believe, live on in history as one of the most remarkable incidents of the war. On Christmas Eve we were in a line of advance trenches waiting to be relieved. It was dark when we heard singing and shouting coming from the other trenches at right angles to us. The news filtered down. German and English officers had exchanged compliments and agreed on a truce. Then we started giving one another a concert. We sang every song we could think of."

Lance-Corporal R. S. Coulson
London Rifle Brigade

"I have just been through one of the most extraordinary scenes imaginable. Tonight is Christmas Eve and I came up into the trenches this evening for my tour of duty. Firing was going on all the time. Then about seven the firing stopped. I was in my dugout reading a paper, and the mail was being dished out. It was reported that the Germans had lighted their trenches up all along our front. We started calling Christmas wishes to one another. I went out and they shouted 'no shooting,' and then somehow the scene became a peaceful one. All our men got out of the trenches and sat on the parapet, and the Germans did the same, and they talked to one another in English and broken English. I got on top the trench and talked German, asking them to sing, and they did. Then our men sang quite well, and each side clapped and cheered for the other. I felt I must sit down and write the story of this Christmas Eve before I went to lie down. If I get through this war alive, it will be a Christmas to live in one's memory." (His letter, dated Christmas Eve, was written to his wife.)

Captain R. J. Armes
1st North Staffs

"I gazed at the scene all around: the stillness, the stars, and the now dark-blue sky. From where I stood I could see our long line of zigzagging trenches and those of the Germans as well. Songs began to float up from various parts of our line."

Charles Bruce Bairnsfather
1st Warwickshire's 2nd Lieutenant

voices crying, 'English solders, English soldiers, Happy Christmas. Where are your Christmas trees?' And faint but clear, the songs of the season accompanied their voices."

Carl Muhlegg, a private at Ypernbogen near Langemarck, remembered fifty years later: "I handed the captain the little Christmas tree. He lit the candles and wished his soldiers, the German nation, and the whole world 'Peace according to the message from the angel.'"

Hugo Klemm remembered the too-good-to-be-true sight and noted "as far as the eye could see lighted Christmas trees were appearing to the right and left along the whole sector."

Candles, clamped to evergreen branches, flamed with a "glow of light falling everywhere."

"It was a sight I shall never forget," wrote Private W. Weir of the 18th Hussars. And from Gustav Riebensahm, a commander in the Westpahlian Regiment, came this memory: "One had to look again and again to believe what was happening."

German leaders had transported Christmas trees—"tiny tannenbaums"—by the thousands to the frontlines as gifts to their soldiers, hoping to bring them a little holiday cheer. All along the Western Front these trees then became a key component in initiating the truce in many places. Troops watched in "fascinated excitement" as more and more candles, perfectly visible, were lit.

Private Frederick W. Heath's recollection, as published in the *North Mail* newspaper in January 1915, read: "The night closed in early, and the ghostly shadows that haunted the trenches came to

Image left: German government officials solicited donations from the general public to purchase Christmas gifts for serving soldiers. Gifts included tobacco, pipes, and Christmas trees. The poster read: "Christmas in the Field! 1914 Donate Gift Packages for our Warriors!"

> *"It was a truce at which the whole world will wonder."*
> Bernard Brookes
> Queen's Westminster Rifles

keep us company as we stood to arms. Under a pale moon, one could see the grave-like rise of ground which marked the German trenches two hundred yards away. Fires in the English lines had died down, and only the squelch of sodden boots in the slushy mud, the whispered orders of the officers, and the call of the wandering wind broke the silence of the night. The soldiers' Christmas Eve had come at last, and it was hardly the time or place to feel grateful for it. Memory in her shrine kept us in a trance of saddened silence. Back home somewhere in England, fires were burning in cozy rooms and, in fancy, I heard laughter and the thousand melodies of reunions on Christmas Eve. With my overcoat thick with wet mud, and my hands cracked and sore with the frost, I leaned against the side of the trench and, looking through my binoculars, fixed my weary eyes on the German trenches. Thoughts surged madly in my mind, but they had no sequence, no cohesion. Mostly they were thoughts of home as I had known it through the years. Still looking and dreaming, my eyes caught a flare in the darkness. A light in the enemy's trench was so rare at that hour that I passed a message down the line. I had hardly spoken when light after light sprang up along the German front. Then, quite near our dugouts, so near as to make me clutch my rifle, I heard a German voice. There was no mistaking it. With ears strained, I listened, and then, all down our line there came to our ears a greeting unique in war: 'English soldier, English soldier, a merry Christmas, a merry Christmas!' Following those words, there

Vintage German postcard from World War I

boomed the invitation from those voices: 'Come out, English soldier; come out here to us.'"

Soldiers from the 2nd Bedfordshires from Britain recalled a German who spoke fluent English coming across No Man's Land in the darkness, shouting: "I am a lieutenant! Gentlemen, my life is in your hands, for I am out of my trench and walking toward you. Will one of your officers come out and meet me halfway? I am halfway across now, alone and unarmed. Gentlemen, I am waiting. Will not one of you come out and meet me?"

Those looking on from the trench opposite were baffled and bewildered at this soldier, fully exposed, who risked himself.

They watched him increase his advance into the neutral ground running parallel between the adversaries. He had unhesitatingly abandoned his shelter and moved beyond the razor sharp barbed-wire entanglements into the open.

Rifles were readied. The target, visible and vulnerable, was sighted in. Everyone held their breath, waiting to see what would happen.

Silence followed. No attempts were made to gun the man down, and soon it became obvious to everyone's eyes that peace—in a visible form—was on the move.

Entrenched occupants listened to the persuasive word—"Come!"—which was shouted with a sweep of this stranger's arm. And thus bidden, they came.

"There was no firing," wrote Wilbert Spencer, a British soldier who spoke fluent German. "So by degrees each side began gradually showing more of themselves. Can you imagine? Both sides came out, met in the middle, shook hands, wished each other compliments of the season, and had a chat. It was a strange sight between two hostile lines."

"The ground between the trenches was swarming with men and officers of both sides who were shaking hands and wishing each

Vintage German postcard from World War I

other a happy Christmas," recalled Dougan Chater, one of many who experienced those moments firsthand. Historians estimate that 100,000 soldiers participated in the truce in one way or another along the front.

"The first man I came to was an old man, and when we shook hands I thought he was not going to let my hand go," wrote Private C. Hunter of the 2nd Monmouthshires. "The tears came rolling down his cheeks, and I felt so sorry for him as he was old, and just wanted to go home."

Aggression was absent, and soldiers, justifiably startled, stared at the sight of their weaponless rivals emerging from beneath the ground as they "came nearer" across the cratered landscape where explosions had shuddered the earth and crumbled their dirt walls. Danger seemed to disappear as the warring nations crossed paths.

"What a sight! Groups of Germans and British extended almost the length of our front," remembered Corporal John Ferguson, a Scotsman. "Where we couldn't talk the language of the other we were making ourselves understood by signs, and everyone seemed to be getting on nicely."

A letter, bearing the signature of Lance Corporal Cooper of the 2nd Northamptons, told of the curious camaraderie: "Now who would believe it if they had not seen it with their own eyes? It is hard enough for us to believe, and we were there."

Sergeant Alfred Lovell, serving Britian, was equally astonished: "Even as I write this I can scarcely understand what I have seen and done. Indeed, it has been a most wonderful day."

From all sides they gathered, these peacemakers, on the transformed battlefield to participate in the impromptu truce. Trenches were vacated by those weary of war. Enemies "pressed hands" with one another in hearty handshakes.

One dozing soldier awoke to find himself alone in his trench, anxious to know: "Where has everyone gone?" He could no longer close his eyes after his question was answered.

German soldiers greeted their French rivals with the words "Bonjour, messieurs," as attempts were made to communicate in the other's native tongue.

"'Come halfways' was shouted back and forth," recalled Corporal John Ferguson. "We were walking between the trenches. At any other time this would have been suicide…We shook hands, wished each other a Merry Christmas, and were conversing as if we had known each other for years. We were in front of the wire entanglements. Soon, most of our company, hearing that I and some others had gone out, followed us…We were laughing and chatting with men whom only a few hours before we were trying to kill."

Lieutenant Frank Black of the 1st Royal Warwicks commented: "We were strolling outside the trenches as though there was no war going on."

The extraordinary moments of mutual armistice began in different ways in different places along the frontlines because of the span of many miles. In some areas, peace was experienced, while elsewhere this was not the case. The truce, which bubbled up from the ranks, became so widespread that "no one was ever certain where or how it began." Specifics varied from unit to unit.

Communal carol singing suspended the conflict on select battlefields during the evening, while in other locations the merry-making commenced on Christmas Day.

A continuous waving of a white surrender flag, elevated by an unnamed soldier who took matters into his own hands, was the first domino to fall in an area served by Lance-Corporal George Ashurst who wrote: "Coming across from the German trench was a solitary man carrying a white flag high above his head."

News of the truce held headlines, including the story of a German

Remembrances

"We were able to move about for the whole of Christmas Day with absolute freedom. It was a day of peace in war."

Private Simnett
1st North Staffordshire Regiment

"It was good to see the Germans standing on top of their trenches, and the English also, with caps waving in the air, all cheering."

Private H. Scrutton
Essex Regiment

"We did not fire that day, and everything was so quiet that it seemed like a dream."

Rifleman J. Reading

"The silence was extraordinary. From all sides birds arrived, and we hardly ever see a bird generally. Later in the day I fed about fifty sparrows outside my dugout, which shows you how complete the silence and quiet was."

Lieutenant Edward Hulse

"Altogether we had a great day with our enemies, and we parted with much handshaking and mutual goodwill."

Percy Jones
Queen's Westminster Rifles

"I have never seen such a sight! I shall remember it to my dying day."

Sergeant A. Lovell
3rd Rifle Brigade

"Believe me, it was worth seeing."

Corporal Laird

soldier who suddenly appeared in No Man's Land, venturing with a lit Christmas tree lifted dramatically above his head. He beckoned to the soldiers in the fortifications opposite. Reporters called this sight "the light of peace," and told how the illuminated tree triggered a swift succession of mingling and merriment from troops eager to respond.

"We marched forward like Father Christmas with parcels hanging from us," wrote Hugo Klemme, recalling the festive scene. "All was quiet. No shooting."

Occupants from both sides proceeded out of their trenches in equal readiness, without hindrance, waving outstretched arms. Spirits buoyed, and the neutral ground was quickly—and thickly— populated with troops walking to and fro during the advancing tide of brotherhood.

Generous gestures followed. Soldiers unwrapped gifts sent from home and shared them with their adversaries during the reprieve. Rifleman A. E. Watts remembered trading "mince pies, Christmas pudding, almonds, and raisins" during the ceasefire.

"We ate their sauerkraut," wrote Charles Smith of the 6th Cheshires, who served near Bailleul, "and they ate our chocolates and cakes."

The first headline to appear in an American newspaper was published by the *New York Times* on New Years Eve and read: "Foes in Trenches Swap Pies for Wine."

Coffee, cheese, and tea were sampled during these Yuletide visitations. It was as if the soldiers forgot what they were fighting for. Kurt Zehmisch of the 134th Saxons commented in his diary: "Thus Christmas, the celebration of love, managed to bring mortal enemies together as friends for a time."

Instead of bracing themselves against an attack, they embraced their enemy; instead of shooting, they shook one another's hand. The only thing shot during those memorable episodes were photos.

World War I Christmas illustration

Caption read: "Christmas plum pudding is mighty good stuff and will be hailed with delight in the trenches. It is good to know that arrangements have been made whereby every man on active service will receive his share of pudding this Christmas day."

With our best wishes for
Christmas 1914

May God protect you and
bring you home safe

Mary R   George R.I.

Everyone was rounded up "like guests at a wedding" for group images.

Names and addresses were scribbled on bits of paper, and promises were made to write after the war ended.

Jams and jellies were traded, along with nuts and newspapers, socks and scarves, mufflers and mittens. These articles of comfort had been knitted and crocheted by mothers and grandmothers.

"An enemy officer presented one of our officers with a scarf as a token of gratitude for his care of their wounded," remembered George Paynter, a 2nd Scots Guard. "That same evening, a German orderly came to the halfway line and brought a pair of warm, woolly gloves as a present in return. The donor was Major Thomas. He had just received them as a Christmas gift."

Tobacco products were also exchanged during the unlikely encounters. Germans found themselves smoking British cigarettes (sent to the troops by the daughter of King George and Queen Mary of England), and British soldiers puffed on German cigars and pipes (sent to the front lines by German leaders). Gifts from ruling officials and imperial authorities were enjoyed by the enemy.

Germans brought out bottles of schnapps, Scotsmen broke open bottles of rum, and the French uncorked wine and champagne.

Barrels of beer followed. Aidan Liddell of the 93rd Argyle and Sutherland Highlanders wrote to his parents: "This afternoon the Germans rolled two barrels of beer into our trenches!"

Captain C. I. Stockwell, an English officer, noted: "The Germans were shouting, 'Don't shoot. We don't want to fight today. We will send you some beer,' and a barrel was hoisted above the trench. Three men came hurrying, rolling it into the middle of No Man's Land.

Image left: Queen Mary and King George sent a holiday postcard to all of their soldiers.

'You had better take the beer,' they urged. 'We have lots.' So I called up two men to bring the barrel to our side. I did not like to take their beer without giving something in exchange, and I suddenly had a brainwave. We had plenty of plum puddings, so I sent for one and formally presented it to him in exchange for the beer."

Uniform accessories also changed ownership. Belt buckles, badges, and buttons were cut from coats and trousers. These items were pocketed, stowed away as lasting reminders of that remarkable Christmas. Never for a moment thereafter could those who were there doubt their participation.

Joint burial services were held later in the evening in abandoned buildings near the frontlines. "We fixed up a sort of makeshift altar in a barn," remembered Robert de Wilde, a Belgian artillery officer. "From a nearby village, in ruins, we fetched a few candleholders, a missal, a pyx, and an altar-cloth."

Wine bottles, now empty, served as candleholders for solemn services in unlikely chapels where prayers ascended for those who were no more.

"Chaplain Adams arranged a reading of the 23rd Psalm," recalled Arthur Pelham-Burn, 2nd Lieutenant in the 6th Gordon Highlanders. "An interpreter wrote the words out in German. First they were read in English by our padre, and then in German by a boy who was studying for the ministry. It was an extraordinary and most wonderful sight. The Germans formed up on one side, the English on the other, with the officers standing in front, every head bared. Yes, I think it is a sight one will never see again."

"They brought the dead man, laid him on the ground, and each of us laid a handful of earth upon him as we prayed the Lord's Prayer together," wrote Captain Joseph Sewald of Germany's 17th Bavarian Regiment. "One of their officers, a captain, clasped his hands together and looked towards heaven and said, 'My God, why

World War I devastation

cannot we have peace and let us all go home?'"

Major Murdock McKenzie Wood wrote years later: "I have come to the conclusion that I have held very firmly ever since, that if we had been left to ourselves there would never have been another shot fired. For a fortnight the truce went on. We were on the most friendly terms, and it was only the fact that we were being controlled by others that made it necessary for us to start trying to shoot one another again." Major Wood eloquently summarized his contemplations and remained as certain of his conclusion as he was of anything.

For a "fortnight" peace continued in some places, and in other places it lasted even longer. Lance-Corporal Hender of the Royal Engineers reported on December 26: "This turned out to be another day of peace. About 10:00 a.m. some German troops came forward and I honestly think they wanted to surrender. They came within hearing distance and kept shouting, 'Me come with you,' but our officers sent them all back."

Lance-Corporal Bell of the London Rifle Brigade spent part of December 28 in what was left of the roof of a bombarded house on sniper duty. He wrote in his diary: "Owing to the truce there is nothing to do. We can all see the fraternization going on." He commented on December 30: "Truce continues. Most amazing.

> *"When the history of the war is written, one of the episodes which chroniclers will seize upon as one of the most surprising features will undoubtedly be the manner in which the foes celebrated Christmas. How they fraternized in each other's trenches—played football, rode races, held sing-songs, and scrupulously adhered to their unofficial truce—will certainly go down as one of the greatest surprises of a surprising war."*
>
> *South Wales Echo* newspaper
> January 1, 1915

Starting with the 'peace and goodwill' idea on Christmas Day, it was found so mutually pleasing that neither side, though keeping a close watch, fires a shot." A secondary entry on December 30 was included: "A German officer opposite to us expected a visit from a general, and said he would be opening fire between 11:00 and 12:00, and we had better keep our heads down."

Lieutenant J. D. Wyatt recalled the same message being passed among his comrades. "We were told to keep down because they might have to do a little shooting at us to make things look right. After all, this is war."

The German newspaper, *Plauener Sonntages-Anzieger*, reported: "The English are shooting randomly into the blue."

The Germans were echoing the efforts of their opponents, firing skyward, beyond the treetops, engaged in a fictitious artillery duel, "wasting ammunition in trying to shoot the stars down from the skies."

Major Buchanan-Dunlop wrote to his wife on December 27, 1914: "Such a curious situation has arisen on our left. The Germans all today have been out of their trenches and had tea with our men halfway between. They only fire four shots a day. Two of their officers and seventy men came into our trenches and have refused to return. They insist on staying."

An "unexpected visitor," a German soldier with a beer bottle in each hand, showed up in a British trench occupied by the London Rifle Brigade on New Year's Eve hoping to wish his "English friends" a "Happy New Year." Graham Williams, an English soldier who was present, recalled: "We managed to heave him up out of the trench. Then two of us each took hold of his arms and led him back across No Man's Land. He was between us, staggering along, singing a song at the top of his voice, until we reached the German barbed wire where there was a gap which he had obviously come through.

I said to the other chap: 'I don't think we'll go any further; if we get into their trench they might want to keep us there.' So we headed the German in the right direction, wished him a Happy New Year, and left him."

When Vize-Feldwebel Lange of the XIX Savon Corps was given the order to resume hostilities, he protested: "I can't fire! They are good fellows. I can't!" His reluctance was met with stern disapproval.

Command-level officers turned on those who refused to do as they were told and, in an acid response, demanded, "Fire—or we will… and not at the enemy!"

Soldiers were verbally pounded by their superiors and, duly warned, they took heed. Weapons previously laid down were picked back up. (It's hard to argue with a gun pointing at your head.) Fierce fighting erupted, and the earth trembled. The truce was over and done with.

Peace evaporated like a puddle in the sun, and the frontlines quickly returned to a place where peace could only be found in a grave.

Many of those who witnessed the truce, those who took "a final look around" and "waved farewell," never again could hear the carol "Silent Night, Holy Night" without feeling their cheeks wetting. Until the evening of their days, thoughts of those Christmas Eve serenades persisted, and the rememberers were hastened back to battlefields where they had walked, once upon a time, among shell holes during those hours uninterrupted by gunfire.

There, in the glow of stubby candles, the supremacy of peace had presented itself, a peace some believed Christ presided over. Letterwriters used the word "holy," in a shared feeling of awe, as if knowing, deep down, God's hand had been extended as surely as their own there on the Western Front in a place called "No Man's Land," which became Every Man's Land during the dramatic

HERE'S WISHING YOU A HAPPY
CHRISTMAS AND A SAFE RETURN

Image above*:* Christmas postcard sent by Britain's General Smith-Dorrien, 1914

Prior to the outbreak of World War I, General Smith-Dorrien remained unconvinced that war was necessary. He visited a training camp for British cadets and declared: "The war should be avoided at almost any cost. It would solve nothing. The whole of Europe—and more besides—would be reduced to ruins, and the loss of life would be so large that whole populations would be decimated."

Donald Christopher Smith, one of the three thousand cadets present, was shocked to to hear the general's speculation. He later wrote: "In our ignorance, I and many of us, felt almost ashamed of a general who uttered such depressing and unpatriotic sentiments, but during the next four years, those of us who survived the horror—probably not more than one-quarter of us—learned how right General Smith-Dorrien's prognosis was, and how courageous he had been to utter those words." The young cadet openly confessed the error of his arrogant conclusion.

It is unknown if Smith-Dorrien offered input to the military order dated December 19, 1915, which read: "The Brigadier wishes you to give strictest orders to all ranks: Any man attempting to communicate with the enemy wither by signal, or by word of mouth, or by any other means, is to be seriously punished. All snipers and machine-guns are to be in readiness to fire on any Germans showing above the parapet." Regarding the truce of 1914, it was noted: "NOTHING OF THE KIND IS TO BE ALLOWED ON THE FRONT THIS YEAR."

invasion of brotherhood. There, they had stood at tables—dusty, makeshift altars—"prepared for them in the presence of their enemies," and there, goodness and mercy followed.

"It was the simple impulse of human souls, drawn together in the face of a common and desperate plight," wrote the editor of *The Scotsman* newspaper who put pen to paper on January 8, 1915. "Those of us who are left at home may well think of the Christmas truce with wonder and thankfulness. The men who kept it proved, as men will always prove when the challenge is given with sufficient directness, that the human soul stands out, quite simply, a thing of infinite goodwill."

> Merry Christmas
> Frohe Weihnachten
> Joyeux Noel
> Vroliijk Kerstfeest

"Christmas in the trenches! It must have been sad, do you say? Well, I am not sorry to have spent it there, and the recollection of it will ever remain one of imperishable beauty."

A Belgium Soldier

"I am a different man today because of who I was that night. Was I a hero? Ah, for just one night, yes. We were all heroes."

Francis Tolliver

Melody and Merriment Ringing in the Trenches

World War I Christmas illustration

Caption read: "Under the muzzle of their guns, wreathed with holly and mistletoe in honor of the Christmas festival, four soldiers of the heavy artillery lift their voices, and their carols rise toward the stars that are shining equally on battlefields abroad as they are on peaceful fields back home."

A CHRISTMAS CAROL.

IN PROSE.

BEING

A Ghost Story of Christmas.

BY

CHARLES DICKENS.

WITH ILLUSTRATIONS BY JOHN LEECH.

LONDON:
CHAPMAN & HALL, 186, STRAND.

MDCCCXLIII.

A CHRISTMAS CAROL

Charles Dickens, England's most celebrated Victorian novelist, wrote his immortal classic, *A Christmas Carol*, in 1843. The book, released December 19, sold out in four days. Laman Blanchard, a reviewer at the time, assured readers the masterpiece would be "remembered for a hundred Christmases to come," and his comments proved prophetic. By the close of the nineteenth century, *A Christmas Carol* was the "second most known Christmas story in the world," following Christ's Bethlehem birth, and no other book had sold more copies except the Bible.

By 1943, President Franklin Delano Roosevelt was reading Dickens's outstanding achievement—his "noble," "heart-softening," "exquisite gem"—aloud at the White House, as he had done annually since taking office eleven years earlier during the Great Depression. The president was comforted by Dickens's enduring words which were written on behalf of "the poor man's child."

The author chose to use his genius to personally respond to a report he read detailing child labor abuses in factories and mines. "My heart so sinks within me when I go into these scenes," he confessed after traveling to witness the suffering firsthand, "that I almost lose hope of ever seeing them changed."

Little could Dickens have known how his message-laden text in defense of the defenseless—his "new gospel," as others came to refer to it—would inspire benevolence in individual hearts across the world, from the common man to royal monarchs.

The Queen of Norway, so moved by Dickens's plea within the *Carol*, sent gifts to London's crippled children and signed each tag: "With Tiny Tim's Love."

"I have endeavored in this ghostly little book to raise the ghost of an idea, which shall not put my readers out of humor with themselves, with each other, with the season, or with me. May it haunt their houses pleasantly, and no one wish to lay it aside."

Their Faithful Friend and Servant, C.D.
December 1843

Charles Dickens opened *A Christmas Carol* with a personal message expressing hope that his "ghostly little book" would "haunt" his readers "pleasantly." And this it did, with epic success.

The beloved storyteller wove his "ghost of an idea"—his reminder that we have a moral obligation to help those who are unable to help themselves—into his narrative. His persuasive argument on behalf of the deprived and despaired, the diseased and discarded, did not fail to find an audience.

Charles Dickens
Portrait by Francis Alexander, 1842

At first glance, several of Dickens's characters—the Ghosts of Christmas Past, Present, and Yet-to-Come, along with a chain-rattling Jacob Marley—appear to be more appropriate for Halloween than Yuletide. However, as the attention-holding plot develops, the conjured apparitions are pointedly effective in delivering their Christmas message.

Dickens's strategically-placed words, spoken through specters, carried the power to cut readers to the marrow of their bones, and then propel their souls soaring. Intermingled observations embedded within the text revealed both the glory of man and its absolute opposite. Within Scrooge, readers could glimpse their own selves—their potential and their shortcomings.

The poet Thomas Hood described *A Christmas Carol* "with its opulence of good cheer" as being "impossible to read without a glowing bosom and burning cheeks between love and shame for our kind."

The book opens with a lengthy description of Ebenezer Scrooge, among literature's most memorable characters:

> *Oh! But he was a tightfisted hand at the grindstone; a squeezing, wrenching, grasping, scraping, clutching, covetous old sinner! Hard and sharp as flint; self-contained, and solitary as an oyster. The cold within him froze his old features, nipped his pointed nose, shriveled his cheeks, made his thin lips blue. He carried his own low temperature always about with him. External heat and cold had little influence on him. No warmth could warm, nor wintry weather chill him. No wind that blew was bitterer than he.*

Thus begins the narrative description of the snarly miser who was stingy on good tidings and generous on "bah, humbugs." But then, only one night, and several ghostly visitants later, Ebenezer, in the final scene, is jubilant, changed for the better—renewed and

Marley's Ghost.

First edition illustration by John Leech, 1843

restored, revived and redeemed, a repentant man:

> *"I am as light as a feather, I am as happy as an angel, I am as merry as a schoolboy!...A merry Christmas to everybody! A happy New Year to all the world!"*
>
> *...He went to church, and walked about the streets, and watched the people hurrying to and fro, and patted children on the head, and questioned beggars, and looked down into the kitchens of houses, and up to the windows, and found that everything could yield him pleasure. He never dreamed that any walk—that anything—could give him so much happiness!*
>
> *...And to Tiny Tim, who did not die, he was a second father. He became as good a friend, as good a master, and as good a man as the good old city knew, or any other good old city, town, or borough in the good old world. Some people laughed to see the alteration in him, but he let them laugh, and little heeded them, for he was wise enough to know that nothing ever happened on this globe, for good, at which some people did not have their fill of laughter at the outset...His own heart laughed, and that was quite enough for him.*

Dickens's influential message, delivered through the characters he made live, kept a firm hold on readers and reminded them that we are here for one another, collectively responsible for the welfare of our world.

Robert Louis Stevenson, the literary great, after reading two of Dickens's Christmas books, *A Christmas Carol* included, wrote to a friend: "I cried my eyes out and had a terrible fight not to sob. But oh, dear God, they are good, and I feel so good after them. I shall do good, and lose no time. I want to go out and comfort someone—I shall give money. Oh, what a thing it is for a man to have written books like these to fill people's hearts with pity."

Lord Francis Jeffrey, editor of the *Edinburgh Review*, offered his approving nod as well: "Blessings on your kind heart, my dear

Dickens," he wrote. "We are all charmed with your *Carol*. Chiefly, I think for the genuine goodness which breathes all through it, and the true inspiring angel by which its genius has been awakened." He lauded further: "You may be sure you have done more good, and not only fostered more kindly feelings, but prompted more positive acts of beneficence, by this little publication, than can be traced to all the pulpits and confessionals in Christianity since Christmas 1842."

Reviewer Laman Blanchard embraced Dickens's *Carol* completely, saying it was for young and old—both—with its message of Christmas, yes, but also "for every season, whether the sun shines or the snow drifts."

Praise flooded forth without hesitation from others who called the *Carol* "a rich Christmas offering," a "benevolent work," a book of "surpassing beauty," "substantial truths," and "next to the Bible, a valuable textbook for old age."

According to Brian Sibley, *Carol* historian, "Dickens saw the festival as embodying not just a commemoration of the nativity of Christ, but the whole of Christ's life and ministry." Dickens summed up his willful intent: "I meant a good thing."

Since then, the *Carol's* words have not been rendered obsolete, even after nearly two hundred years—quite to the contrary. Old Ebenezer's crotchetiness and irritability show up on stages and television screens near and wide, followed by his transformed life, as the holiday approaches. Opportunities abound to hear Scrooge's nephew, Fred, define the season:

*"I have always thought of Christmastime, when it comes round...
as a good time: a kind, forgiving, charitable, pleasant time; the only
time I know of in the long calendar of the year when men and women
seem, by one consent, to open their shut up hearts freely, and to think
of people below them as if they really were fellow passengers to the*

Etching of children working in mines
(included in the 1842 "Children's Employment Commission" report)

grave, and not another race of creatures bound on other journeys. And therefore, Uncle, though it has never put a scrap of gold or silver in my pocket, I believe it has *done me good, and* will *do me good, and I say God bless it!"*

Dickens used his characters to speak truths he held within his own heart. When the imaginary Fred—"a most accurate and literal description of Dickens"—delivers his good-natured outburst, readers are witnessing the personhood of the author himself whose son, Henry, remembered the holiday in his household as "a great time, a really jovial time, and my father was always at his best, a splendid host, bright and jolly as a boy, throwing his heart and soul into everything that was going on."

Mamie Dickens, Charles's daughter, wrote in 1897: "Christmas was always a time in our home which was looked forward to with eagerness and delight, and to my father it was a time dearer than any other part of the year. He loved Christmas for its deep significance, as well as for its joy."

A Christmas Carol confronts its audience with scenes of unsurpassed celebration, and then contrasts them against visions wholly heartbreaking.

Dickens used his *Carol* to respond to two disgraceful reports from the "Children's Employment Commission." These reports are the "how" and the "why" the manuscript came to be written. The first report, released in 1842, exposed societal toxicity and widespread abuses to children laboring in mines—tin and coal—and was illustrated with half-naked, boney youngsters toiling strenuously in their desperate circumstances. The follow-up report, released in 1843, informed the public how oppressed youth, shouldering burdens inescapable and unendurable, were struggling six days a week in London factories and sweatshops prevalent during the industrial revolution.

Dickens, sickened, was deeply moved by the inclusion of word-for-word accounts from actual flesh-and-blood laborers like Emily Pennington, age 16, whose matter-of-fact reality was summarized: "Has been an apprentice as a milliner two years and three-quarters; is boarded and lodged; in the winter season she begins to work at half-past 7:00 a.m. and leaves off about 11:00 p.m. if they are not very busy; occasionally she goes on until 12:00, not later; in the summer she begins at half-past 6:00 a.m. and leaves off about 1:00 in the morning; has sat up until 2:00 a.m. or 3:00 a.m.; has never worked all night."

Eighteen-hour workdays were not uncommon for those like Emily whose back was bent, statue like, postured over a sewing machine, even though the law limited a child, nine years of age and older, to work a maximum of twelve hours per day.

Children were legally hired at the age of nine and given meager rations of both food and rest. For countless, hope was a word that did not exist. Their childhood ended barely before it began, snuffed out like a candle at day's end.

"I am so perfectly stricken down by the book you have sent me," wrote Dickens to Parliament Commissioner Dr. Thomas Southwood Smith, "that I am thinking of writing, and bringing out, a very cheap pamphlet called 'An Appeal to the People of England on Behalf of the Poor Man's Child.'"

Dickens's initial intent was then set aside a few days later. In follow-up correspondence he told Dr. Smith that he had "reasons for deferring the production of that pamphlet until the end of the year. I am not at liberty to explain them further just now, but rest assured that when you know them, and see what I do, and where, and how, you will certainly feel that a sledgehammer has come down with twenty times the force—twenty thousand times the force—I could

Charles Dickens
Sketch by Daniel Maclise, 1843

Bob Cratchet and Tiny Tim
Wood engraving by Solomon Eytinge, Jr., 1867

have exerted by following out my first idea." That "sledgehammer" blow was *A Christmas Carol*.

On the evening of October 5, 1843, Charles Dickens delivered a passionate speech at a charity gathering in which he expressed his wish to take those within his hearing to the places he had visited, places of extreme wretchedness and undiluted suffering where, he told his audience, "my own heart dies within me when I see thousands of immortal creatures condemned, without alternative or choice."

Afterward, Dickens wandered the shadowed streets of Manchester. Words and faces began to take shape in his mind. These images and ideas later found their way into the pages of *A Christmas Carol*. Bob Cratchit appeared, hoisting his crippled son, Tiny Tim, onto his shoulders, as did two charity collectors who attempted to kindle kindness as they solicited a donation from Old Ebenezer:

> *"At this festive season of the year, Mr. Scrooge," said the gentleman, taking up a pen, "it is more than usually desirable that we should make some slight provision for the poor and destitute who suffer greatly at the present time. Many thousands are in want of common necessaries; hundreds of thousands are in want of common comforts, sir…A few of us are endeavoring to raise a fund to buy the poor some meat and drink, and means of warmth. We choose this time because it is a time, of all others, when want is keenly felt and abundance rejoices."*

Jacob Marley emerged in phantom form from within Dickens's fertile imagination. The ghostly visitant, shackled in chains and moaning exceedingly, walked through a bolted door to warn Scrooge that we are all chained to the error of our choices. He lamented:

> *"Why did I walk through crowds of fellow beings with my eyes turned down, and never raise them to the blessed star which led the*

wise men to a poor abode? Were there no poor homes to which its light would have conducted me?"

Scrooge moved forward and backward in time through Dickens's mind as well, eventually heeding Marley's warning in a cemetery before being returned to his bedroom where his stone-heartedness melted away and new-found insight surfaced:

The bedpost was his own. The bed was his own, the room was his own. Best and happiest of all, the time before him was his own, to make amends in!

"I will live in the past, the present, and the future!" Scrooge repeated, as he scrambled out of bed. "The spirits of all three shall strive within me. Oh, Jacob Marley! Heaven, and the Christmas time be praised for this! I say it on my knees, old Jacob, on my knees!"

Dickens, in truth, was haunted by his characters and "saw" them. Members of the Cratchit family made their presence known.

"They were ever tugging at my coat sleeve," said Dickens of the experience, "as if impatient for me to get back to my desk and continue the story of their lives." Like a returning echo they came with their urgings, day after day, and, because of this, the undertaken task was completed in a whirl, in less than six weeks.

"I was very much affected by the little book myself and was reluctant to lay it aside for a moment," wrote Dickens to his friend, Charles Mackary. "I walked aimlessly about the black streets of London, fifteen and twenty miles, many a night, when all the sober folks had gone to bed."

Dickens "wept and laughed and wept again, and excited himself in a most extraordinary manner in the composition," remembered Georgina Hogarth, the author's sister-in-law.

When completed, Britannia praised the book's merit and Dickens's "sympathy for human suffering…not for the imaginary and fictitious distresses, but for the real grinding sorrows of life." Another observer commented that such sympathy for the impoverished "cannot easily be attained by those who have not lived the life of the poor."

Readers were moved by the narrative's authenticity. The text resonated with truthfulness. It was as if Dickens knew, actually knew, what undiminished despair felt like. And, secretly, he did.

Dickens, unbeknownst to his readers, was a man who was as familiar with the life of a pauper as he was with the life of the privileged, but he forbade his biographer from disclosing the private pain he had lived through as a child until after his death. Very few were aware that Dickens labored in the company of rats, clawing out their existence, in a wretched factory where he pasted labels on bottles of shoe polish after his father and mother were arrested and thrown into debtors prison, condemned for their inability to pay their bills.

"Its wainscoted rooms, and its rotten floors and staircase, and the old gray rats swarming down in the cellars, and the sound of their squeaking and scuffling coming up the stairs at all times, and the dirt and decay of the place, rise up visibly before me," wrote Dickens to his biographer (for later inclusion in his life story), "and it is as if I were there again. My whole nature is so penetrated with the grief and humiliation of such considerations that even now I often forget in my dreams that I have a dear wife and children, even that I am a man, and I wander desolately back to that time in my life."

These memories—predatory and parasitic—clung to Dickens like flesh, wounds that refused to heal, wearing and tearing upon his plagued mind. "No words can express the secret agony of my soul as I sunk into this companionship," confessed Dickens, the Dickens "no one knew."

His naked honesty revealed his intimacy with suffering. He

lived it, felt it, recognized its stench, and heard its sound as he toiled in the grime and soot of that abhorred place where his spirit was broken beyond repair. His soul, completely assaulted by the inhumane and appalling conditions it encountered while listening to the conversations of rodents, was left unable to erase away its remembrance of being filthy, hungry, and alone on the other side of those barred prison windows.

"I know how all these things have worked together to make me what I am," confessed the writer of his hidden history, "but I never afterwards forgot, I never shall forget, I never can forget." For Dickens, the clock kept spinning its hands backward, reversing time, returning him to the past, failing his attempts to bury those reoccurring memories. Until his hair grayed, he watched them crawl out of their shallow graves, over and over, unearthing themselves, and knew they would only be permanently buried when he was.

He was affected, disturbingly so, and because of this, Dickens remained ever mindful of the distraught, unable to turn his back on them.

In 1843, before and during the composition of *A Christmas Carol*, Dickens had reason to weep while inking those blank pieces of paper. His fortunes were falling, his fame was fading, his debts were deepening, and the carefree days that companioned him at the peak of his success had gone astray—snatched away. His wife was pregnant with their fifth child, and she knew the taste of moldy bread. The family, debt-burdened beneath pressing financial obligations, found it necessary to borrow money in order to pay bills.

Fear, breathing down Dickens's neck, stalked him on those twenty-mile walks past hooting owls and the Marshalsea prison with its bricked walls and rusted padlocks. He looked upon it, moonlit, in a nervous sweat, visibly shaken, overwhelmed by anxiety, uncertainty, embarrassment, and pain, wondering if history was on the verge of

Scrooge and Marley's ghost
Scrooge, 1923 film

repeating itself in this next generation.

As the threat came nearer to Dickens's door, he was unable to put his mind at ease, nor distance himself from his intruding remembrances. His confidence sagged, and he believed, beneath the surface, that he had lost his talent for writing. "I have the wrong kind of fire burning in my head," he confessed, "and I don't think I can write."

Thank God he was wrong, and the unveiling of *A Christmas Carol* proved it.

The impact of "the little book" was immediate and intense. Readers, both the nameless and the well-known, responded eagerly to the author's "spellbinding powers" as they passed their copies from hand to hand after the publication sold out in four days, by

First edition illustration by John Leech, 1843

December 23. Another printing was rushed through, and a third was ordered before New Years. Since then, the book's pages have remained open and the novel has never been out of print.

G. K. Chesterton, a Dickens biographer, declared that *A Christmas Carol* was created in "that great furnace, the heart of Dickens," and added, "the story sings from end to end like a happy man going home."

Within two short months of the *Carol's* release, eight different theater companies in London produced adaptations of the story on their stage. It was a number that eventually doubled.

At one of the later productions, an interesting incident occurred. The food used for the Cratchit family's Christmas feast kept disappearing—even half a goose! The mystery was solved soon thereafter when it was learned that the young girl who played Tiny Tim at the theater was passing plates of applesauce, potatoes, and plum pudding through the fireplace prop on stage to her starving sister, hiding behind it, who then took the food home to their famished family. Dickens was saddened when he was made aware of the circumstances and asked: "Why did you not give her the whole goose?"

The author's *Carol* of 1843 arrived at a time when Christmas no longer held prominence in England—nor many places elsewhere, including America. England's holiday observances had actually been outlawed—yes, outlawed—in the mid-1600s when Oliver Cromwell, a Puritan, took control of the government and abolished Christmas.

Parliament, under Cromwell's rule, condemned celebrations in the 1640s, but the harshest decree was issued on Christmas Eve, December 24, 1652. It read: "No observance shall be made of the five and twentieth of December, commonly called Christmas Day, nor any solemnity used or exercised in churches upon that day in respect thereof." Violators faced imprisonment.

Churches were closed, and businesses remained open, with labor not lessened. Gone were the "golden days of yore," and Christmas, waved away, was turned into "a Good Friday." The old customs and celebratory practices were seen as "wicked"—even mince pie—and were quickly denounced and distained, unmaintained.

Cromwell and his anti-Christmas ordinances were eventually ousted when King Charles II, successor to Cromwell, gained power and restored Christmas (or at least tried). The Puritans, however, had demanded such a significant departure from the holiday with their constraints that it became a mere shell of what it had been. In some places, Christmas not only dwindled when it fell into disfavor, it disappeared.

Then along came Dickens who is credited with "rescuing" Christmas with his "greatest little book in the world." In the strokes of his pen, he "breathed new life into the holiday" with scenes of merriment and music, dancing and dining, puddings and pies, and bountiful blessings from long ago. Dickens, a man who "knew how to keep Christmas well, if any man alive possessed the knowledge," wanted the *Carol's* descriptive use of language and jovial imagery to pay tribute to the blazing light of mankind's most joyous hours. And this it did. *A Christmas Carol*, on a grand scale, became a compass with its "God bless us, everyone" message.

For the first two hundred years of America's history, Christmas was barely observed, with "no formalized celebration of the holiday by church or state throughout New England." The holiday wasn't even given official attention on the United States calendar until 1870. Thus, Christmas had not "come and gone" in America, it simply had hardly come because the Puritan rulings of the 1600s coincided with the arrival of our first settlers, Puritans among them.

As Yule scholar Stephen Nissenbum points out, from 1659 until

First edition illustration by John Leech, 1843

1681 there was a Puritan law on the Massachusetts Colony books that forbade the practice of observing Christmas. A fine of five shillings was levied upon anyone caught in the act. It was illegal to sing a Christmas carol, exchange a gift, or even light a candle in recognition of the season.

Christmas remained a "relatively minor affair" in America as late as 1843 because of the Puritan clampdown, but the *Carol's* influence brought changes during succeeding years.

Charles Dickens traveled to America to present many readings of his beloved work in shortened form. His persuasive prose was easily adapted for these stage performances in which the novelist portrayed each of his characters with skillful execution. He was a distinguished orator, and theater tickets sold out quickly. Audiences were moved to tears by Dickens's riveting delivery of the *Carol's* text. In Boston on December 2, 1867, weeping attendees pulled out so many white handkerchiefs that it was reported the following day: "It looked as if a snowstorm had somehow gotten itself into the hall." The "whole house rose and cheered! The people looked at him with gratitude as to one who held a candle to light a dark way."

In the congested crowd that evening were some of America's greatest talents: Henry Wadsworth Longfellow, James Russell Lowell, and Oliver Wendell Holmes. "They hung upon every word that fell from his lips," commented the *Boston Journal* the next morning.

Franklin Fairbanks, a manufacturer from St. Johnsburg, Vermont, and owner of the Franklin Scale Company, attended one of the Boston performances with his wife who noted that her husband's face "bore an expression of unusual seriousness" as the author threaded his way through the layered truths within the *Carol*.

Afterward, Fairbanks confided to his wife: "I feel that after listening to Mr. Dickens's reading of *A Christmas Carol* tonight that I should break the custom we have hitherto observed of opening the

Charles Dickens
Wood engraving by *The Illustrated London News*, 1870

works on Christmas Day."

Fairbanks found himself pondering what was forfeited by his workers against the lesser value of what he gained by it, and in the spirit of a reformed and charitable Ebenezer, Fairbanks used the Scrooge "of the final pages" to transform his life and change his ways. From then on, the Franklin Scale Company was closed on Christmas Day and every factory worker was sent home with a turkey for his family, a most-pleasing gesture which was initiated after the owner's heart was seized—and swiftly lifted—by a man named Dickens whose book "of opposites" brought him face-to-face with his own self.

Such was the power of the *Carol*. It introduced matters both ethical and moral through characters like the lame child Tiny Tim, clinging to his crutch, and the emotionally crippled Scrooge who was spiritually handicapped.

Dickens, the persuader, boldly examined the attitudes he believed deformed us and presented Tiny Tim as the healthier character because within him beat a heart "not in need of repair."

In the end, Scrooge, the wealthiest and most pitied man in the story, came to understand that he had everything, yet nothing in terms of what really mattered—love, peace, joy, contentedness. These could not be counted amongst his belongings before the punctual appearance of the intervening phantoms.

This same tactic of confronting audiences with a redefinition of wealth was used in the Christmas classic "It's a Wonderful Life." Old Man Potter, "the richest man in town," was a character wealthy only in dollars, a character who failed to be the hero of his story for he never came to understand that life's ultimate assets have nothing to do with accumulating balances in bank accounts. Scrooge, on the other hand, did. He chose change, knowing full well that he could not alter what had been, but he could alter what would be.

With renewed interest in everything and everyone, an invigorated Scrooge threw open his bedchamber window, and his soul opened with it. Dickens wrote of the scene: "Golden sunlight! Heavenly sky! Sweet, fresh air! Merry bells! Oh, glorious, glorious!" The new day brought new life for the converted Scrooge who resolved to live within the realm of charity, mercy, and benevolence.

Shelved volumes of Dickens's authorship have lived on—and rightfully so. His invincible messages remain with us, especially his belief that the suffering of our fellows is a "shame upon us all." His pen was motivated by his empathy for the abandoned.

At the writer's passing, England's Queen Victoria noted in her diary: "He is a very great loss. He had a large, loving mind and the strongest sympathy with the poorer classes."

A lowly laborer learned of Dickens's death while walking the London steets and muttered, "We have lost our best friend."

The London Times announced Dickens's passing by saying he was the "great apostle of the people" who "touched their hearts with his creations, familiar to every man, high or low," and the *New York Times* predicted on the same day that the name of Charles Dickens would "be spoken with gratitude and affection as long as our language endures."

The *Globe and Traveler* offered the notable opinion that *A Christmas Carol*, although so short, was "his most touching work, and there are few men who have not felt better, and more kindly disposed towards humanity at large than they ever felt before when they have read, or still better yet listened to Charles Dickens reading, the exquisite pathos of Tiny Tim's contented but suffering life." Thomas Carlyle expressed admiration for his friend who he remembered as "the good, the gentle, high-gifted, ever-friendly, noble Dickens; every inch of him an honest man."

Dickens, this "poet of the poor," was eulogized at his funeral by the Reverend Dean Stanley who called *A Christmas Carol* the "finest charity sermon in the English language." He believed countless souls had profited by the passages within it.

Dickens's grave was dug inside the prestigious Westminster Abbey, the cathedral of kings and queens. It was, in truth, the last place in the world the writer would have wanted to be laid to rest. He left explicit instructions for his body to be buried in a common way, like a common man's, in "an inexpensive, unostentatious, and strictly private manner" with "no memorial erected," and a plain headstone carrying nothing but his name. The people, however, "decreed otherwise."

They placed his remains in the Poet's Corner of the magnificent cathedral, in the eternal company of literary greats like William Shakespeare, Rudyard Kipling, Jane Austen, William Blake, Charlotte Bronte, Robert Browning, and William Wordsworth, entombed and memorialized beside him.

Thousands of mourners poured into the cathedral over ten consecutive days, overflowing the church. As they left, a printed memorial message was placed in their hands. It read: "Charles Dickens was a sympathizer of the poor, the suffering, and the oppressed, and by his death one of England's greatest writers is lost to the world."

His body was lost, but his words remained.

"Words are the only things that last forever; they are more durable than the eternal hills."

William Hazlitt

Sheet music, 1870

THE "THANK YOU TREE"

The citizens of Boston, Massachusetts receive a Christmas tree each holiday from the Canadian city of Halifax, located in the Nova Scotia province.

The evergreen is a gift, sent as a gesture of continuing gratitude to commemorate the noble service Halifax received from Boston during its blackest hours following the worst man-made, accidental explosion in world history on December 6, 1917, nineteen days before Christmas.

The *Boston Post* newspaper ran its first headline one day after the disaster. It read: "Boston Rushes Relief! Trainload of Physicians, Nurses, Red Cross Workers, and State Guard Officers on Way to Halifax."

The entire eastern seaboard was alerted to the tragedy after random telegraphs were forwarded from station to station, sounding the alarm. Within two hours of the blast, Governor Samuel W. McCall of Massachusetts was reading the following telegraphed message which had been keyed at a railway station three miles outside of the stricken community: "Organize a relief train and send word to Wolfville and Windsor to round up all doctors, nurses, and Red Cross supplies possible to obtain. No time to explain details, but list of casualties is enormous."

Governor McCall's response was immediate. By evening's end on December 6, 1917, train whistles in Massachusetts were blowing and a final "all aboard" was being shouted. Boston was on its way, without delay, with an urgently needed human cargo.

The train, headed due north, was filled to the bursting point with supplies and medical professionals whose faces were among the first to arrive in Halifax. The compassion they gifted to the sufferers of that slain city during the Christmas season of 1917 was a gift that was held in the heart instead of the hand.

Nearly one hundred years have passed since the first "Thank You Tree" was delivered to Boston in December of 1918 to acknowledge appreciation for the support Boston offered to Halifax during its trial by fire the previous year. The tree's arrival today represents both a time-honored tradition of thankfulness, as well as a pilgrimage into the past.

Faded-ink newspapers of yesteryear tell us that it took only minutes for Halifax, a bustling capital and military community, to be turned into a city with sorrows to spare.

On the morning of December 6, 1917, passersby greeted one another with the words "beautiful day," and it certainly was, at least until the sky turned from blue to black.

Approximately eighty ships lined the harbor at dawn. Some were empty, others full, loaded with soldiers bound for World War I battlefields. Halifax was a critical wartime city at that time and a major supply line. According to historian Mary Ann Monnan, Novia

HORRORS OF HALIFAX UNEQUALED IN WAR

Harrowing Scenes Surpass Any On Battlefields, Says Survivor

Frenzied Men Rush About Wildly in Search Of Lost Loved Ones

The Boston Globe, December 8, 1917

The New York Times.

MUNITION SHIP BLOWS UP IN HALIFAX HARBOR, MAY BE 2,000 DEAD;
COLLISION WITH BELGIAN RELIEF VESSEL CAUSES THE DISASTER;
TWO SQUARE MILES OF CITY WRECKED; MANY BURIED IN RUINS

The New York Times, December 7, 1917

THE PITTSBURGH SUN — FINAL

MANY PERSONS KILLED AND INJURED WHEN MUNITION-LADEN SHIP BLOWS UP AT HALIFAX; FLAMES SWEEPING CITY

The Pittsburgh Sun, December 6, 1917

Scotia had the highest enlistment record of any province in Canada, and all transported troops passed through the Halifax port. The city was also an international maritime haven for ships from neutral countries.

A six-mile channel known as "the narrows" ushered crafts into the harbor and caused, at times, congested vessel traffic. Such was the case during the dreaded hours of that "never-to-be-forgotten" December day.

Two ships, the *SS Imo* and the *SS Mont Blanc*, were on a collision course with one another in the thinnest point of the lane. Attempts were made by their captains to steer clear and avoid contact. Engines were reversed, but these efforts were insufficient. Impact became inevitable, and everyone who had their eyes turned toward the harbor knew it.

What was not known was that one of the ships, the French *Mont Blanc*, was carrying 400 tons of TNT and 2,300 tons of a highly volatile picric acid for use in the war. The crew had neglected, however, to raise a red flag, the universal symbol for "I Have Explosives on Board."

The *Mont Blanc* arrived in Halifax the night before from New York where it had been loaded with bulk ammunitions. It became a "floating bomb," a destroyer, capable of rendering a death sentence on anyone in its path.

The empty *Imo*, a four-masted Norwegian steamship bound for New York to pick up relief supplies for the country of Belgium, plowed into the *Mont Blanc* and ripped the vessel open at approximately twenty minutes to nine. Sparks flew and flames ignited. Torn drums of benzene and picric acid were set ablaze in a cataclysmic chain reaction. The result was similar to lighting an enormous stick of dynamite, and twenty-five minutes later the dynamite boomed.

Firemen rushed to the scene as the first flames gathered, and

Vincent Coleman

curious townsfolk, completely unaware of the deadly potential in their midst, wandered down to the water's edge to watch the events unfold.

Witnesses on the docks noticed frenzied crewmembers on board the *Mont Blanc* deserting their ship in a furious haste and rowing "like madmen" away from their abandoned vessel. Once ashore, they ran in the opposite direction of the waterfront. A bystander who survived remembered one of the Frenchmen yelling to the mostly English-speaking crowd something that sounded like: "Powder! Powder!"

Vincent Coleman, a train dispatcher for the Canadian Government Railways, was also running. He fled his telegraph-dispatch office with his co-worker, William Lovett, when a panicked naval officer alerted them that one of the ships involved in the collision was carrying a deadly cargo and was going to blow. Coleman turned around and returned to his post when he remembered that an incoming train with 300 passengers on board was due to arrive in Halifax shortly.

His heroic message read: "Hold up the trains. Ammunition ship on fire in the harbor making for pier number eight. Will explode. Guess this will be my last message. Goodbye, boys." Coleman was fully aware that death, for him, was holding all the aces.

His lifeless body was found in the flattened building where his last words were typed, words which saved the life of every passenger on board the halted train, but not his own.

At exactly four minutes and thirty-five seconds after the clocks in Halifax tolled nine, Vincent Coleman perished as the *Mont Blanc* was vaporized.

The only damage suffered on the spared train, four miles away, were smashed windows, blown out from the force of the "great roaring noise" which stunned the ears of those on board.

1,630 homes were destroyed in totality in an instant, and 12,000 more were damaged. 9,000 citizens were injured, and another 6,000 were left homeless. 25,000 more were without adequate shelter. The death toll was officially tallied at 2,000, but unofficially it was believed to be closer to 3,000, including those listed as "never found."

Window panes were shattered as far as fifty miles away by the concussion wave that followed, as was reported by the "National Geographic" magazine in their article documenting the Halifax disaster. Dishes fell from shelves at eighty miles when a "feeling of wind" passed across the land. The explosion was felt 130 miles to the north, and heard 220 miles to the east. A rumbling "roll of thunder" caused listeners on a clear day to pause and ask: "What was that?"

"That" was a detonation of such unimaginable horror that it tore Halifax asunder and turned its shoreline into an inferno. A great column of fire reached heavenward, and a dark mushroom cloud billowed out around it, spread across the sky on all sides of the piercing shaft of light, a suspended "black umbrella." Beneath, a rain of airborne debris fell: soot, glass splinters, shrapnel, and limbs—

from trees and bodies. The beautiful morning had ended.

So ferocious was the unfathomable power of the blast that some survivors were left naked when the pressure wave of air ripped the seams on their clothing open. William Wells, a fireman who barely had time to unroll his hoses, gave graphic testimony of his experience: "The force of the explosion had blown all of my clothes off as well as the muscles from my right arm."

The devastation was immediate, and Halifax came unhinged. Trees snapped in half with severe suddenness, and rooftops were peeled back. Walls shook. Buildings were lifted off of their foundations and dropped in an agitated order. Steeples toppled and tumbled as brick-and-mortar structures were reduced to rubble. Brass bells rang—and no one pulled on their ropes. Harbor waters were blown away, thrown seaward, and the floor beneath was exposed. Great piles of debris were heaped high as incomprehensible wreckage was wrought in a span of mere moments.

Then came the tidal wave which returned the displaced harbor

Grove Presbyterian Church

waters to their original location and added another sixty feet to the high-water mark on the already-crippled city. Citizens who survived the flames were drowned in the deluge.

Sixteen inches of snow followed within twenty-four hours. Survivors beneath the rubble froze to death as a result of the blizzard's onslaught, unable to answer the hoarse voices calling out their repeated names. "All Rescue Work at a Standstill in Howling Blizzard," announced the headline which appeared in the neighboring *Calgary Daily Herald* on December 7. Those who remained alive, wounded and weary, found themselves filled with an all-permeating sense of dread.

On Sunday, December 10, 1917, the *Morning Chronicle* newspaper printed their first summary of the calamitous scene under the heading "The Disaster in Brief." The article beneath read:

> *Over 2,000 persons believed to be dead. 73 bodies recovered Sunday. Portion of the city from the waterfront west on Russell Street, north on Gottingen Street to the narrows is completely devastated—two square miles. Twenty thousand persons destitute and homeless. One thousand bodies recovered to date. Hospitals and other large buildings filled to overflowing with wounded, many of the cases having since died. Relief is being rushed from various parts of Canada and the United States. The first relief train to arrive reached Halifax on Saturday afternoon from Boston, bringing a corps of doctors, surgeons, and Red Cross nurses, under the direction of the Honorable A.C. Ratschesky, the personal representative of Governor McCall of Massachusetts. Search for bodies among the ruins of buildings continues, and the death toll is hourly growing. Large buildings in the devastated section are all a mass of smoking ruins.*

A charred Halifax was in vital need of blankets, bandages, glass sweepers, doctors, chisellers—to carve names, numbers, and angels

Image right: Halifax in ruins

into slabs of granite—and men with shovels to bury stacked-high coffins.

Boston, the largest American metropolitan city nearest to Halifax, was singled out in the *Morning Chronicle* article for its rapid response to pleas.

Governor McCall of Massachusetts forwarded a telegram to Halifax's mayor within two hours of the blast. It read: "Understand your city is in danger from explosion and conflagration. Reports only fragmentary. Massachusetts ready to go the limit in rendering every assistance you may be in need of. Wire me immediately."

No response was received because wires were down. This prompted a second message from the governor sent via wireless communication: "Since sending my telegram this morning offering unlimited assistance, an important meeting of citizens has been held, and Massachusetts stands ready to offer aid in any way you can avail yourself of it. We are prepared to send forward immediately a special train with surgeons, nurses, and other medical assistance, but await advices from you."

Again, no reply arrived, and Governor McCall sent one final sentence: "Realizing that time is of the utmost importance, we have not waited for your answer but have dispatched the train."

The hastily assembled medical unit, gathered on a Boston train depot platform, was given the order to board. Departure was swift, but arrival in Halifax was delayed because the relief train was unable to maneuver through the deep snows covering tracks along the way. A manual dislodgement was necessitated.

A second train departed Boston on December 7 carrying necessary equipment for a complete hospital, including seven hundred cots and seven thousand blankets. A shipload of private donations from Boston citizens arrived next carrying everything from boots to 1,100 gallons of milk.

Relief workers were hardly prepared for the intimidating aftermath which faced them when they finally found their way to Halifax. Skeletal buildings were lying in confused disarray on the ground. Other structures, still standing, were torn open with their innards exposed. Lampposts were horizontal instead of vertical. Victims were being transported in wheelbarrows and tin bathtubs to makeshift hospitals where they were propped up against walls until beds could be set up. The wreckage was both emotional and material.

Hardly a window pane in all of Halifax remained whole, and eyes embedded with broken glass shards were in urgent need of surgical attention.

Survivors nailed rugs from the floor over windows on the wall to halt snow from drifting into their homes further. Some were blind. They had lost their sight, but not their lives, and wished to secure some sense of order.

Members of the Massachusetts Safety Committee were alerted to the immediate need for glass, and they sent it. Maine, too, readied a cargo containing 200,000 panes and 10,000 rolls of tar paper. Their state hospital unit was also sent.

Rhode Island likewise mobilized a medical unit. Their team "responded to the appeal for help so promptly that they forgot to bring any red cloth for their Red Cross armlets," remembered Bernard Gow, a Canadian who assisted as a volunteer alongside them. "On the railway journey to Halifax they cut up the green curtains on the train to make armbands and became known locally as the Green Cross."

New York sent prefabricated houses to provide temporary winter quarters in their rally to aid Halifax. Significant contributions were generated in every corner of the United States, with New England communities representing a prominent physical presence in Halifax.

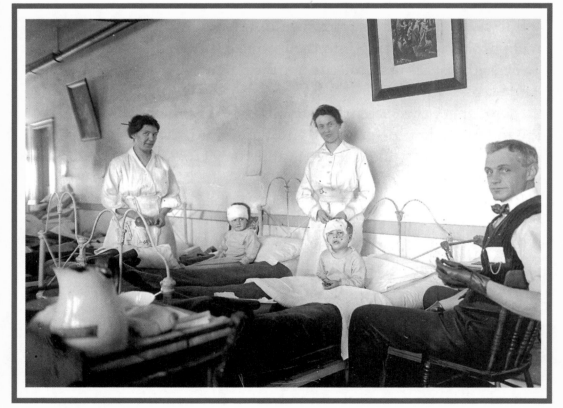

American medical personnel

In particular, Boston's "errand of mercy" was most prevalent.

A poem written by Clark Hall summed up Canada's gratitude: "When good old Boston heard the news, she answered like a flash; and sent us food and clothing—likewise, men and cash. As soon as they received the news, without the least delay, they got their trains in readiness, and started on their way. God bless our neighbors to the south, God bless them one and all; they responded so magnificently to humanity's urgent call. Wherever the spangled banner floats, on water or on land, you'll always find them ready to reach out a helping hand."

Halifax officials on the relief committee exercised meticulous care in recording the outpouring of charity. All gifts—from the smallest to the largest—were noted by the recipients. A $50,000.00 donation from British Columbia was recorded next to an anonymous gift from "a little girl" in the amount of three cents. Each was given recognition and was valued.

A donation from a paperboy named Lewis Hickey living in Palo Alto, California was recorded at $19.00. He and his fellow sixth-grade students hoped to shoulder some of the burden. His letter, received December 14, 1917, read:

To the Mayor of Halifax

My Dear Mr. Mayor,

I sell newspapers before and after school. One evening I read of the dreadful disaster that nearly destroyed Halifax. I felt very sorry when I thought of the people without homes. The next day I asked our school principal at the Lytton Avenue School if the children might not help some of the homeless children of Halifax. She is sending the money to you. I hope it will help you some.

Yours truly,
Lewis Hickey

The list of donations received from U.S. cities and citizens is endless. A few examples include:

Readers of the *Omaha Daily News*, $500.00
C.R. Wright, Frankton, Indiana, $5.00
Town of Enfield, Connecticut, $195.26
Boys Zion Church, Louisville, Kentucky, $11.00
Bishop and Company, Honolulu, Hawaii, $1,000.00
Immanuel Danish Lutheran Church Ladies Aid, Racine, Wisconsin, $10.00
"A patriotic Maury County farmer," Columbus, Tennessee, $25.00
City of Walla Walla, Washington, $275.80
Presser Foundation, Philadelphia, Pennsylvania, $1,000.00
First National Bank of Wyoming, collection, $144.50
H. Choate and family, Winona, Minnesota, $100.00
Boston Insurance Company, Boston, Massachusetts, $50,000.00
"A Texas barber," collection, Dallas, Texas, $5.00
Miss Louise Thrall, Chicago, Illinois, $1.00
Chamber of Commerce, Kansas City, Missouri, $5,000.00
Mrs. Marjorie Solon, Tenafly, New Jersey, $5.00
American troops on board transport ship, $2,110.08
Dr. Albert A. Wells, Ashville, North Carolina, $10.00
"A friend," Wilmington, Delaware, $2.00
City of Chicago, Illinois, first payment, $50,000.00

Chicago added an additional $200,000.00 to their initial amount. ($1.00 in 1917 would be equivalent to $20.00 today.) Mayor Thomson's note, written on behalf of the people of his city, acknowledged Halifax's earlier gift to Chicago after their "great fire," a gift which remained a permanent part of their remembrance. "Halifax was among the first to assist us after our 1871 fire," wrote the mayor, "so Chicago should return the kindness."

Image right: Surviving Halifax children attend a Christmas party

The letter below, dated February 11, 1918, is on file at the public archives in Nova Scotia, Canada. The correspondence was addressed to the *Care Yale* newspaper in New Haven, Connecticut.

Dear Sir:

In acknowledging your letter of February 3, I wish to express to you—and all those associated with you in the splendid contribution of clothing for the aid of sufferers here—our very sincere thanks for the thoughtful and tangible expression of sympathy. I am afraid that I am hardly competent to write a news item for your publication which would be suitable, and which would adequately describe conditions existing in Halifax immediately following the catastrophe of December 6, but the following paragraphs will, I trust, be of some personal interest.

Thursday, December 6, 1917 was a beautiful, clear fall day, scarcely a cloud in the sky, no wind, and just that tang in the atmosphere such as one likes to feel in football weather. At 9:00 a.m., laborers and mechanics were at work in various parts of the city. Clerical help and employees in various business places were either already at their posts or hurrying to get there, and business and professional men were in some cases still at the breakfast table, reading the morning paper or leisurely strolling down to their offices, when just like the snap of a whip, there came a rumbling—a pause—then a terrific roar which shook the entire city from one end to the other, and what had been a peaceful well-ordered community was changed in the twinkling of an eye into a mass of wreckage and shattered humanity.

No words can begin to describe the scene that followed. With 2,000 people killed outright, another 5,000 or 6,000 seriously injured, many of whom where blind as a result of flying glass, and an additional third of the population more or less badly cut, the memory of that eventful day is not a pleasant one to look back upon.

Almost immediately the whole northern district of the city was in flames, and with the report that another explosion was likely to occur, the population of that badly devastated district who could still run or walk, streamed south and west in an attempt to reach some open place where they felt they would be safe. Hysterical mothers and fathers looked for their children who had been killed as they sat at their desks in school. Practically everyone had blood streaming from terrible gashes in the face and head as they rushed hither and thither in a vain attempt to save some of their belongings or rescue some of their family or friends…

With the night, snow came and the first real touch of winter. The agony and suffering of the next forty-eight hours cannot be described in any way. Hospitals were so overcrowded that one could scarcely walk without treading on some poor, unfortunate human wreck. Houses were so badly shattered that it was impossible to keep out the weather. And the storm, increasing to a blizzard, brought about a crisis that tried the nerve of the strongest man.

Within an hour after the explosion, emergency relief had been established at the City Hall with Robert T. MacIlreith as Chairman. Associated with him was a small band of public citizens who had, in some miraculous manner, escaped serious injury. For the following ten days and nights these men stayed at their post without thought of their own homes or dear ones, in many cases without sleep or a change of clothing, snatching a bite to eat as the opportunity might occur, and working constantly organizing the various branches of relief work, cabling and telegraphing for assistance, supplying the destitute with housing accommodations, food, and clothing, and generally playing their part as heroes in one of the greatest tragedies the world has ever known.

In spite of the almost insurmountable difficulties, communication was kept up, and within the first twenty-four hours food depots were established all over the city. Clothing depots opened and emergency shelters were provided where thousands of destitute were housed. Hospitals with a normal capacity of hundreds were forced to extend their capacity to provide for thousands. At the end of the week a tremendous organization of voluntary workers, running with the smoothness of a well-oiled machine, were taking care of the various requirements of the situation as efficiently as if it had been in operation for years.

Relief came to the stricken city from all parts of the world. Our neighbors in the great nation to the south performed magnificent service by rushing doctors, nurses, surgical supplies, food, clothing, and money to our assistance as fast as trains, steamships, and wire could be pressed into service. The great Commonwealth of Massachusetts is deserving of particular mention in this regard, since by Sunday morning, December 9, they had landed in Halifax a special train bringing nurses, doctors, and hospital equipment galore. Subsequently, they contributed in goods and money to the extent of more than three-quarters of a million dollars and have left no stone unturned to provide in every way possible for the comfort and assistance of those rendered homeless and destitute by the terrible disaster.

Some day the story may be written, and when it is, the outside world will perhaps get some little inkling of what will probably go down in history as one of the tragic happenings of the greatest war the world has ever known…

Sincerely yours,
Ralph P. Bell, Secretary Relief Commission

The Canadian poet Wilber Forrest Davidson wrote:

> And from across the border
> came the voice from Uncle Sam,
> saying, "Hold on up there Halifax,
> we're coming on the land!"
> And when you meet these good people,
> please don't you be shy;
> put your hands across the border
> and lift the "Stars and Stripes" up high!

Material gifts arrived as well. A telegram dated December 17 was received from Brighton, Massachusetts and read: "Friend wishes to contribute toys for one hundred blind children. To whom shall we send them?" Another telegram sent from Boston on December 11 asked: "Would clothing for fifty small boys and girls be acceptable and useful?"

The local newspaper in Colorado Springs printed the following editorial under the heading "REMEMBER HALIFAX!"

> *Let us pack a box for Halifax. Let us prove that the great heart of Colorado Springs beats in sympathy with the stricken people of the north.*
>
> *Let us show them that we are real neighbors; that America is a true friend!*
>
> *Winter is upon them—winter with its biting winds, swirling snow, and freezing cold. It finds thousands of them homeless, foodless, and without clothes. It finds families broken up by death in its most fearful and sudden coming. It finds hearts aching, and lives shadowed with bitter sorrow.*
>
> *It finds poor widows with small children crying for something to eat. Houses which were theirs are now heaps of blackened wreckage.*
>
> *We must give them fuel and food, medicine and clothing, to keep*

them alive, and other things to comfort and cheer. And we must not forget the children. Santa Claus must visit every home in Halifax. That will be our Christmas gift to them.

A letter from the relief committee in Halifax, expressing gratitude, was sent to say "thank you" to America, their "neighbors in the great nation to the south," who, by their prominent presence, ably assisted and "performed magnificent service."

An anonymous, eye-witness account of the disaster, dated December 28, 1917, is on file in the archives of St. Patrick's School and Convent in Halifax. It reads, in part: "My first thought was of 'the crack of doom;' my second, that we were being bombarded from the air, or shelled from the sea. I called out, 'Run to the basement!' The children heard only, 'Run!' There was no screaming, just a blind drive without protection through a thick storm of crashing glass, plaster, blackboards, doors, and statuary. The explosion was over before we were downstairs, but the continuous falling of large pieces of furniture prolonged the impression that some sort of attack was still in progress. We went to the yard after a few moments. We had scarcely reached the house when soldiers rushed through the city with the warning that another explosion was expected to follow and that the people were ordered to seek the nearest places of safety since the houses would undoubtedly succumb to this second shock. The entire surviving population went quickly. There were infants from the Foundling Asylum, each borne lovingly in the arms of the sisters or the soldiers who had come to their rescue; there were panic-stricken children from the Institute for the Deaf; there were the aged, the sick, the dying; priests, laity; Catholic, Protestant; rich and poor; every class distinction nullified, every antipathy forgotten in the wave of sympathy and fear which united all hearts. There were births and deaths in these open places of refuge during the horrible hour of suspense. The hospital to which I went was so closely packed that it was almost impossible to pass between the bodies. Death was there in various forms—some had been drowned by the great waves from the parted waters, some burned by the powder and pitch, some mangled by splintered glass, or wounded by large pieces of iron from the ship. One mother seeking her little boy found him with both his eyes blown out. His first words as he took her hand were, 'Mama, it is night.'"

Regarding the grand assembly of Americans who converged on Halifax's doorstep, the anonymous woman wrote: "I wish you could hear the blessings which the poor and suffering are invoking on the Americans. Surely, the United States is the great, warm heart of the world. On the morning after the arrival of the first relief train from the States, I went into the hospital to a poor man whose eyes had been terribly injured. He had been in despair. Now, he grasped my hand saying, 'Sister, I am going to be all right. There's a Yankee nurse looking after me, and, I tell you, she knows her business.' *That* was the beginning of an endless chain of gratitude."

The "chain" spoken of by the unknown writer continues to this day. It is linked to the perennial presentation of the "Thank You Tree" in Boston, an evergreen which commemorates the fused relationship between these two "sister cities," a relationship which began when doctors and nurses boarded Halifax-bound trains to deliver dusk-to-dawn care to sufferers who were looking to the horizon for help from beyond their borders. The example of all of those who served reminds us that caring for one another is life's supreme effort.

And may others come to know these words are true because of you.

Editorial cartoon, *The Evening Mail*, Halifax
The caption read:

Thanks, Sam!
Your heart is as big as your country is broad!
You have Canada's heartfelt gratitude.

Saint Nicholas's Golden Gift

Saint Nicholas has been traveling the world for nearly eighteen hundred years on a journey which began in the coastal village of Patara in the ancient land of Asia Minor, mountainous country bordered by three seas—the Aegean, the Mediterranean, and the Black.

Since his birth in approximately 280 A.D., Nicholas's name has been carried across centuries and continents, literally to "the ends of the earth."

Stories of the Byzantine bishop, who was ordained to his task at such a young age he was nicknamed "the boy bishop," were told by merchants riding on the backs of camels and donkeys through vineyards and olive groves. Mariners likewise shared accounts of Nicholas's remarkable generosity and miraculous deeds as they voyaged in vessels crossing interconnected trade routes. In this way, Nicholas's memory was preserved, and stories of the "gift giver" flourished like a well-watered garden.

Images of a white-bearded Nicholas, wearing his clerical attire, began to appear in visual renderings—statues, paintings, mosaics, and stained-glass windows. Countryside chapels and towering cathedrals were erected and bore his name. Over two thousand were consecrated by the year 1500 A.D., and some of the earlier structures are among the oldest churches in the world.

Gifts given in memory of Saint Nicholas were first recorded in the eleventh century in France where he was the country's patron saint. Early gifts included fruit, nuts, and candy. Greece, the Netherlands, Norway, Sicily, Italy, Switzerland, Scotland, Ireland, and England adopted him as a patron saint also. In Russia, peasants referred to him as Nikolai Ugodnik, "Nicholas the Helper," while in Austria the gift giver was simply known as Niklaus. Italians called him San Nikola, and to the Germans he was Sankt Niklaus. In Dutch homes, Sinterklaas (their agglutination of "Sint Nicolaas") filled shoes with gifts instead of stockings.

As early as December 23, 1773, the New York *Rivington Gazetteer* made a reference to the "anniversary of St. Nicholas, otherwise called Saint a Claus," and New York's *The Spectator* published a holiday piece on December 1, 1815 which began: "Oh, good holy man! Whom we Sancte Claus name."

Tiny tots know the name of Saint Nicholas, the eternal friend of children, by heart. They watch in wide-eyed wonder as stockings are fastened to fireplace mantles and stories are told of his annual visit on the eve of December sixth, the commemoration date of Nicholas's death in 343 A.D.

The saintly bishop's historical comings and goings were spread in their infancy by oral tradition during the final years of Imperial Rome, carried by travelers across the length and breath of Europe in the same way early Gospel stories were shared during a time when written texts were rare. Later, details of Saint Nicholas's life found their way into the writings of medieval and ancient chroniclers— Jacob of Varazze, Andrew of Crete, John the Deacon, Symeon, Eustratios of Constantinople, Michael the Archimandrite, Thomas Aquinas. The poet Dante praised Nicholas's virtues in his *Divine Comedy*, and many of the illuminated "Book of Hours" manuscripts from the Dark and Middle Ages included depictions of Nicholas's

Jolly Old Saint Nicholas

Jolly old **Saint Nicholas**, lean your ear this way;
Don't you tell a single soul what I'm going to say.

Christmas Eve is coming soon, now you dear old man,
Whisper what you'll bring to me; tell me if you can.

When the clock is striking twelve, when I'm fast asleep,
Down the chimney broad and black,
with your pack you'll creep.

All the stockings you will find hanging in a row;
Mine will be the shortest one; you'll be sure to know.

Johnny wants a pair of skates; Susie wants a sled;
Nellie wants a picture book—yellow, blue, and red.

Now I think I'll leave to you what to give the rest.
Choose for me, dear **Santa Claus**, what you think is best.

Anonymous lyrics
(The song possibly dates to the 1860s.)

Saint Nicholas holding a sack of gold
(stained-glass window in Wales)

exemplary, unselfish deeds (in particular, his secret gift of three bags of gold to an impoverished family).

Nicholas, an only child, was orphaned as a young teenager when a sweeping plague infected both of his parents. He then lived under the guardianship of an uncle, a Father Superior in a local monastery, who influenced his decision to train for the ministry. After Nicholas consecrated his life to God, he shed himself of his earthly belongings and gave his entire inheritance away to those in need.

His most famous act of charity was given anonymously in the middle of the night. Legend holds that Nicholas was told about a local father who was in financial despair and planned to sell his three daughters into slavery—or, according to some accounts, prostitution—because no one would marry them without a dowry. (New brides were culturally expected to bring finances into a marriage to set up their household.) Nicholas, learning of the family's dilemma, chose to intervene and save the maidens.

Making his way through the shifting evening shadows along the darkened, deserted streets of Myra to their home, Nicholas concealed his identity in a hooded cloak. Three bags of gold from his bounty, dowries for each of the poverty-stricken daughters, were thrown through an unlocked window. The bags landed in shoes lined up along the floor next to the window. (Some accounts say the gold coins landed in stockings which were hung on the bedposts to dry. Other accounts say the gold, thrown through a smoke hole in the wall, landed in stockings by the fireplace. Still other versions tell how the gold bags were delivered on three successive evenings, or over a longer period of time.)

The cloaked benefactor hurried away, but the father, who had heard a thud and discovered the gold, chased him down. He wished to thank the stranger for his helpful intervention. Nicholas begged for anonymity, and wished for his gift to remain a secret. The grateful father, however, shared the story of his family's plight and Nicholas's willingness to assist them. The story then traveled into the farthest corners of the globe and provided inspiration for our modern-day gift-giving traditions.

Historian William Bennett asks the question: "Why bother with the history of Saint Nicholas?" And he answers: "The larger reason is because he matters to Christmas. This saintly man who lived so long ago influences one of our holiest seasons and most beloved holidays, and this influence, which has come across many centuries, is a kind of miracle. For one thing, his story is fascinating. Its sheer vastness of scale is astounding. It stretches from the crossroads of Europe, Asia, and Africa, to the Americas and beyond. It crosses oceans, deserts, and the frozen arctic. It's an adventure tale complete with emperors, knights, villains, shipwrecks, kidnappings, treasure, and dark dungeons. It is the age-old struggle of good against evil, of right against might. And if the reputation Saint Nicholas left behind means anything, then we know there was something remarkable about this man. For hundreds of years, his name has been invoked and his deeds recounted. His shadow falls across epochs."

Saint Nicholas. He was a flesh-and-blood, living human being with a spirit truly emblematic of the holiday season. He came to represent kind deeds freely given with no expectation of return and is remembered for efforts he extended to lessen the hardships of those around him.

Shelves of books recount his miracles—healing the sick, multiplying grain for the hungry—and although scholars differ in their piecing together of the fragmentary details, they are united in their opinion that Nicholas's life was lived in such a way as to be worthy of example. His name remained among the people long after he left them, a name which literally meant "hero of the people" or "the people's victor."

Saint Nicholas's charity mission
Painting by Fra Angelico, 15th century

BEGINNING A NEW SERIAL BY RALPH HENRY BARBOUR
JANUARY, 1910
St NICHOLAS
ILLUSTRATED MAGAZINE
FOR BOYS AND GIRLS

FREDERICK WARNE & CO · BEDFORD ST · STRAND · LONDON
THE · CENTURY · CO · UNION · SQUARE · NEW · YORK
FRANK H. SCOTT, PRESIDENT   WILLIAM W. ELLSWORTH, SECRETARY   UNION SQUARE, NEW YORK
Copyright, 1909, by The Century Co.]   (Trade-Mark Registered Feb. 6, 1907.)   [Entered at N. Y. Post Office as Second Class Mail Matter

Image above: "St. Nicholas" magazine was the most popular children's magazine in publishing history during its run from 1873 until 1939.

The journey Saint Nicholas took over the distance of time from a remote corner of the crumbling Roman Empire to worldwide recognition is a long one indeed, as well as complicated. The bishop's pilgrimage to America added additional layers to his evolution. The "Santa Claus" we know today is a merger of various Christmas traditions linked to the Old World, as well as inventions in the New.

Several men were primarily responsible for the transformation. John Pintard, a founder of the New York Historical Society, is among them. He included Bishop Nicholas in his 1793 almanac and later named him patron saint of both New York City and the New York Historical Society in 1809. The goodly bishop was toasted at the Society's annual banquet: "To the memory of Saint Nicholas," the members cheered. "May the virtuous habits and simple manners of our Dutch ancestors not be lost in the luxuries and refinements of the present time." Pintard commissioned a woodcut of Saint Nicholas holding a money purse (to represent his famous golden gift) and presented it to all members.

Washington Irving, a young writer remembered for his stories "The Legend of Sleepy Hollow" and "Rip Van Winkle," was at the toasting and was welcomed that evening as a new member. He had just released a book, *History of New York from the Beginning of the World to the End of the Dutch Dynasty*, on Saint Nicholas Day, December 6, 1809, in which he raised awareness of Saint Nicholas "who makes children of us all."

Clement C. Moore joined Pintard and Irving in elevating the bishop with his poem "A Visit from Saint Nicholas," a favorite of youngsters. Moore had been enchanted with Washington Irving's Christmas writings and further inspired by a book published in 1821, *The Children's Friend*, the first lithographed book in America.

The Children's Friend included a reference to "Santeclaus" using a reindeer to pull his sleigh on his trip across the heavens:

Old Santeclaus with much delight
His reindeer drives this frosty night.
O'er chimney tops and tracks of snow,
To bring his yearly gifts to you.

Instead of a single reindeer, Moore provided eight when he composed his poem one year later. He also used Christmas Eve for Saint Nicholas's midnight mission, as did the author of the anonymous lines above, instead of December 6.

In some countries, Saint Nicholas's visit was anticipated on New Year's Day, while in other countries he was looked for on January 5, the eve of Epiphany. (Church calendars recognize January 5 as the date the wise men arrived at the manger with their gifts of gold, frankincense, and myrrh.)

Moore's verses had a profound effect on readers, as well as a significant influence on the holiday as a whole. The poem's initial audience (outside of those within the Moore household) were readers of the *Troy Sentinel* newspaper in upstate New York. The editor of the paper published Moore's stanzas anonymously on December 23, 1823, and offered the following introductory remarks about the unknown author: "We know not to whom we are indebted for the following description of that unwearied patron of children who…goes about visiting the firesides of this happy land, laden with Christmas bounties, but from whomsoever it may have come, we give thanks for it."

The response to the children's ballad was immediate, and newspapers far and wide began reprinting the rhymed lines holiday after holiday until many could recite the readily recognizable words from memory. Two titles were interchanged in the early years of the poem's nearly 200-year existence: "A Visit from Saint Nicholas" and

MERRY CHRISTMAS

COPYRIGHT 1906
L.R. CONWELL, N.Y.

I sprang from my bed like a flash
Tore open the shutters threw
up the sash
When what to my wandering
eyes should appear
But a miniature sleigh and
eight tiny reindeer
With a little old driver so
lively and quick
I knew in a moment it must
be St Nick.

JOLLY CHRISTMAS

St. Nicholas brings pleasure
In bounteous measure,
And I'm hoping you're there
When he calls with your share.

Vintage postcard

"A Visit from Santa Claus." Eventually, "Santa Claus" held favor and the kindly bishop from long ago exchanged his cleric robes for a red velvet coat and trousers trimmed in white fur.

William Bennett offered a notable opinion about the historical meanderings of Saint Nicholas: "The stories of Saint Nicholas and Santa Claus are perhaps not literally true, but they are arguably true in a more important way. They are morally true. They offer generosity, kindness, and self-sacrifice over avarice, cruelty, injustice, and self-indulgence. They are about the celebration of human closeness and decency, and the caring of others. They are about families at the hearth. In their totality, they are about the raising of sight and efforts toward a better life. The image of Saint Nicholas has changed many times through the years and Santa Claus is a part of that evolving image. At his best, he stands for the virtues Saint Nicholas champions: compassion, service, selflessness, largeness of spirit. There is one essential truth in the stories of Nicholas and Santa Claus: the goodness of the gift offered with no expectation of anything in return. The value of three bags tossed through a window does not lie in the gold they contained. The act of giving in itself made those bags priceless. That same spirit lives in our time in a parent or other adult who, with secret joy, watches a wonder-struck child discover on Christmas morning that Santa has paid a nighttime visit. Santa Claus is, in a very real sense, the result of a Christ-inspired goodness that has rippled across seventeen centuries, from Nicholas's time to our own. Despite secularization and commercialization, Santa Claus is a manifestation of Nicholas's decision to give to others. The history of Saint Nicholas and Santa Claus is a kind of miracle in itself. It is a legacy that resonates with God's love."

Santa Claus. "Thank God he lives, and he lives forever," wrote Francis Pharcellus Church in 1898 in the most reprinted editorial in American journalism. Church's words, translated into twenty languages, were written in an attempt to answer a question sent to *The Sun* newspaper in New York by an eight-year-old girl named Virginia O'Hanlon. Her letter, addressed "Dear Editor," read: "Some of my little friends say there is no Santa Claus," she explained. "Papa says, 'If you see it in *The Sun*, it's so.' Please tell me the truth. Is there a Santa Claus?"

Church's reply—"Yes, Virginia, there is a Santa Claus"—was written by a man who had served as a war correspondent on hardened battlefields and who never knew fatherhood, yet his memorable narrative spoke true to the heart of childhood:

> *Virginia, your little friends are wrong. They have been affected by the skepticism of a skeptical age. They do not believe except what they see. They think that nothing can be which is not comprehensible by their little minds.*
>
> *All minds, Virginia, whether they be men's or children's, are little. In this great universe of ours man is a mere insect, an ant in his intellect, as compared with the boundless world about him, as measured by the intelligence capable of grasping the whole of truth and knowledge.*
>
> *Yes, Virginia, there is a Santa Claus. He exists as certainly as love and generosity and devotion exist, and you know that they abound and give to your life its highest beauty and joy. Alas! How dreary would be the world if there were no Santa Claus! It would be as dreary as if there were no Virginias.*
>
> *There would be no childlike faith then, no poetry, no romance to make tolerable this existence. We should have no enjoyment except in sense and sight. The eternal light with which childhood fills the world would be extinguished.*
>
> *Not believe in Santa Claus! You might as well not believe in fairies! You might get your papa to hire men to watch in all the chimneys on Christmas Eve to catch Santa Claus, but even if they did not see Santa Claus coming down, what would that prove?*
>
> *Nobody sees Santa Claus, but that is no sign that there is no Santa Claus. The most real things in the world are those that neither children*

nor men can see. Did you ever see fairies dancing on the lawn? Of course not, but that's no proof that they are not there. Nobody can conceive or imagine all the wonders there are unseen and unseeable in the world.

You tear apart a baby's rattle and see what makes the noise inside, but there is a veil covering the unseen world which not the strongest man, nor even the united strength of all the strongest men who ever lived, could tear apart.

Only faith, fancy, poetry, love, romance, can push aside that curtain and view and picture the supernatural beauty and glory beyond. Is it all real? Ah, Virginia, in all this world there is nothing else real and abiding.

No Santa Claus! Thank God he lives, and he lives forever. A thousand years from now, Virginia, nay, ten times ten thousand years from now, he will continue to make glad the heart of childhood.

"Backward, turn backward, oh, time, in your flight!
Make me a child again just for tonight!"

Elizabeth Akers Aller

A Great Depression
Good Samaritan

America was hardly the place to celebrate a "Merry Christmas" in 1933. The Great Depression was raging, and economic upheaval blanketed the land.

Unemployment rates peaked at 25% nationally, but in industrialized Canton, Ohio, where assembly lines halted, the brutal reality of the downturn was even worse. Jobless men and women accounted for nearly half of the city's population. *Half.* For them, hope had faded from view.

Against this backdrop, a man named Sam Stone stepped forward and placed an anonymous ad in the *Canton Repository* newspaper on December 18, 1933, asking for the "opportunity" to help fifty to seventy-five families celebrate "a merry and joyful Christmas." He used the fictitious name "B. Virdot" and included a temporary mailing address to which to send letters. He then added a promise: "The maker of this offer will remain unknown until the very end."

If a handshake had accompanied the ad, it would have been a firm one. True to his word, Sam Stone went to his grave nearly fifty years later, at the age of ninety-three, with his secret in tact, a secret that would have remained if it had not been for an old suitcase found in a dusty attic twenty-seven years after his passing.

Inside, 150 cancelled checks were discovered, all dated the week before Christmas 1933, and signed by a man who never existed: B. Virdot. The suitcase, decades in hiding, also contained the original letters which had caused the generous-hearted benefactor to double the number of families he chose to assist.

It was a Great Depression story which was anything but depressing.

"From 1929 to 1933 the unemployment rate rose from around three percent to a staggering twenty-five percent, which translated to more than thirteen million people unable to find work. Those numbers didn't account for the millions more who were forced to take pay cuts and reduced hours. Home foreclosures skyrocketed. After taking office in 1933, President Roosevelt tried every trick in the book to jumpstart the economy, but nothing seemed to work. In 1939, more than a decade after the crash, unemployment was still in excess of seventeen percent."

Michael Willian

The Great Depression spanned a decade known as the "Hard Times." Banks collapsed and padlocked their doors. Accounts were wiped out, and families could carry their life savings in a change purse.

Storekeepers hung signs in their windows which read: "Going Out of Business," "For Sale," "For Lease," and "Closed"—not just for the evening, but for good, never to reopen. Buildings fell into disrepair,

Oh, Christmas Tree

Three homeless men, sheltered in a shack, erected a small evergreen next to their makeshift home.

"Let's dance and sing and make good cheer,
for Christmas comes but once a year."

Sir George Alexander MacFarren

and the collective vocabulary of the era included the regular use of words like "bankruptcy" and "eviction."

Bread lines stretched for blocks, and soup kitchens attempted to put a little nourishment in empty stomachs. Americans became accustomed to standing in lengthy lines for food, and even longer lines for employment. Their lives of ease and comfort vanished.

Countless sufferers took up residency in houses made from stacked tires and sheets of scrap metal when the Depression lowered itself across the country like a dark curtain.

In the midst of these trying times, a man named Sam Stone made the decision to help "repair the world," not the whole world, just the world he saw around him every day in his own backyard in Canton, Ohio, where he owned a clothing store downtown, one of the storefronts not yet vacated and boarded up.

Although Stone was a man of means at the time, he was, more importantly, a man who had experienced a plummet from prosperity to poverty during the decade prior. He personally knew what it felt like to be caught in the unyielding grip of a financial stranglehold, and he never forgot it.

For this reason, he sent an anonymous ad over to his local newspaper on December 18, 1933, seven days before the high holiday of mankind. The ad, so small in size he could have covered it up with the hand he used to write it, offered to relieve a bit of burden from a few of his fellows.

When it arrived at the *Canton Repository* office, the editors there, touched by its spirit of goodwill, decided to run a front-page story about it. Their bold headline read: MAN WHO FELT DEPRESSION'S STING TO HELP 75 UNFORTUNATE FAMILIES: ANONYMOUS GIVER, KNOWN ONLY AS "B. VIRDOT," POSTS $750 TO SPREAD CHRISTMAS CHEER. The article beneath went on to detail the mysterious stranger's offer of kindness and his "remembrance of

much darker days."

"This is a genuine Christmas gift," continued the story, "involving no strings, and no embarrassment to the recipients."

The editors were making reference to a promise included in the unknown donor's ad: "To such men or families who request financial aid, the writer pledges that their identity will never be revealed." In summary, B. Virdot's intention was to keep the names of those who requested financial aid a secret. No one would know who requested the checks, and no one would know who sent them. It was a pledge Sam Stone made, and a pledge he kept, all the while hiding his identity from his recipients in plain sight.

The ad's final sentence read: "In writing, please familiarize me with your true circumstances, and financial aid will be promptly sent."

Within a single day, the inflow of letters started to arrive from those overwhelmed by despair, letters signed by families who had maintained a presence in the town since its first bricks were laid. So great was the need expressed in the correspondence received that the ad's offer to send ten dollars to seventy-five families was changed to five dollars in assistance to 150 families.

Five dollars in 1933 would be worth, in today's currency, nearly $100.00. A pound of ground beef sold for eleven cents at the time, and a pound of hot dogs sold for eight. A loaf of bread could be purchased for seven cents, and two dozen oranges cost a quarter. Ten pounds of potatoes were priced at eighteen cents, and cabbage was three cents a pound. Peas were a penny more. The average cost of an American home in 1933 was a mere $530.00.

Many of the recipients of B. Virdot's five-dollar checks immediately sent thank you letters expressing gratitude for the assistance they received, along with notes saying they supported the decision to double the checks and halve the amount in order to help twice as many families.

The downtrodden listened to Bing Crosby croon "Brother, Can You Spare a Dime?" over the radio airwaves during the 1930s. The song topped the charts during the Great Depression and became symbolic of the era.

Ironically, even the minting of dimes was halted in 1932 and 1933 due to the poor economy.

James Brownwell's note, dated December 22, 1933, read in part: "Your fine and much appreciated gift arrived this morning. I hasten to thank you, and say I am in hearty cooperation with your idea of lessening the amount and reaching more needy ones. Accept my sincere thanks with my wishes for many blessings not only this coming Christmas season, but throughout the year."

Rachel DeHoff wrote: "I saw in last night's paper the most human thing I have ever seen in print before…you have chosen the silent way of celebrating Christ's birth…may it never look dark again for you is my prayer." As a young widow, she had become the main artery of her family. The care of her two boys was now her sole responsibility.

"My Dear Mr. B. Virdot," wrote George Monnot, a man who had gone from "owning a thousand cars to owning none" when his dealership in town closed down, "Permit me to offer my sincere thanks for your kind remembrance for a happy Christmas. Indeed this came in very handy and was much appreciated by myself and my family. It was put to good use paying for two pairs of shoes for my girls and other necessities. I hope some day I have the pleasure of knowing to whom we are indebted for this very generous gift."

Sam Stone was a father to three little girls. His ficticious name— "B. Virdot"—was a combination of his daughters' names: Barbara, age one, Virginia, age five, and Dorothy (nicknamed "Dotsy"), age four.

Requests for shoes and clothing appeared again and again. Helen Palm, one of the youngest to appeal to B. Virdot, wrote: "When we went over to the neighbor's house to borrow the newspaper I read your article. I am a girl of fourteen. I am writing this because I need clothing, and sometimes we run out of food. My father does not want to ask for charity, but us children would like to have some clothing for Christmas. We used to have nice things when he had a job. I also have brothers and sisters. If you should send me ten dollars I would buy clothing, and buy the Christmas dinner and supper. I thank you."

Helen Palm's request for clothes and food was echoed by Edith May who pleaded for any "wear and then share" garments that may have been cast off: "If I only had five dollars, I would think I am in heaven," she wrote. "I would buy a pair of shoes for my oldest boy in school. His toes are all out…Have you got any ladies in your family who could give me some old clothes? And, oh my, I know what it is like to be hungry and cold. We suffered so last winter, and this one is worse…Please do help me! My husband doesn't know I am writing, and I haven't even got a stamp, but I am going to beg the mailman to post this for me."

Edith May was without three cents to purchase a stamp to mail her letter, and Helen Palm had borrowed her neighbor's three-cent

1933 three-cent stamps

newspaper publication to read the ad.

Both knew hunger and shivering cold, and both needed shoes they had no money to pay for. Helen had been resoling hers with pieces of cardboard cut from empty boxes of Shredded Wheat cereal.

One letter-writer was wearing shoes in such disrepair he considered himself "almost barefoot," and Ohio was certainly not the place you wanted to be shoeless when winter wrapped itself across the land. There, the thermometer's red line disappears into frigid, single-digit numbers when the calendar page is turned to December.

"My wife has not had a coat in seven years," wrote Howard Sommers, "and her last pair of shoes was bought in 1929." His submitted letter began with the words, "Dear Friend, B. Virdot."

Families caught in the sharp teeth of the Great Depression during Christmas 1933 squared their shoulders and used as little coal and fuel oil as possible when the days grew shorter and whiter. Windows were laced with frost. Snow drifted halfway up the sides of houses and barns. Many dwellings were so cold that those inside could see their frosted breath floating in the air. Blankets and quilts were pulled closer at nighttime, and layers of clothes were worn to bed to help combat brisk temperatures.

It was a time in our nation's history when people went to bed hungry and woke up the same way—a worry most of the younger generation of today can say they never had. The Depression was accompanied by an unprecedented shortage in food because a terrible ten-year drought devastated the agricultural harvests of the entire Midwest in the 1930s. Distressed crops withered and died. Famine took hold of the land. Soil turned to powder and it blew away. The "Dust Bowl" which followed produced storms so black in intensity that they extinguished sunlight from the sky. Farms in the heartland, too numerous to count, were deserted, and their owners defeated. Years passed without a drop of rain—yes, *years*. People felt

Great Depression dust storms—"black blizzards"—devastated farms.

like they were living inside a broken clock. They pulled dandelions from the dry earth and ate the leaves as salad. Hope disintegrated. Then locusts, which thrive in drought conditions, showed up in swarms numbering a billion, eating anything that was left. It was like a plague out of the Old Testament book of Exodus.

The Great Depression was defined by empty cupboards, empty dishes, empty checkbooks, and empty granary bins. By bare shelves and bare bones. By withering flesh and withering spirits. And the letters inside the suitcase, sent to the Kris Kringle of Canton, provided ample evidence of it all. Writers shared details of the lives they used to live, and spoke of a time when a table full of food was a familiar sight. Christmas dinner was now only something to be imagined, and the "good old days" were nothing but a memory.

"You are doing a very good thing," wrote Ruth Aman, whose world had unraveled, "and I wish there were a lot more like you. The people who are lucky enough to have no worry where their next meal is coming from don't realize how it is to be like we are."

Nancy Young told of hardships and misery under her roof. Her penciled words, full of utter broken-heartedness, read: "Dear Sir, I was just sitting in my room this evening looking upon my family, knowing I did not have a cent to my name to even buy them bread, although they were asking about Santa Claus....and I was reading in the paper where you would like to help a poor and needy family out for Christmas. Well I can't get much poorer off than I am."

The down-and-outs who reached for B. Virdot's extended hand summed up their resources as "nil," "like hundreds of others." They turned their empty pockets inside out, to no avail. They lost jobs, homes, businesses, and sometimes even their children because they were unable to provide food for them.

Ida Bailey was one of those who surrendered her malnourished youngsters to the local orphanage, all twelve, but had been able to reunite with four of them. She wrote: "This Christmas is not going to be a merry one for us, but we are trying to make the best we can of it. We want to do all we can to make the children happy, but can't do much. About seven years ago, Mr. Bailey lost his health, and it has been nip and tuck ever since, but we thank God he is able to work again. We all work whenever we can make a nickel honest. Three years ago, this Depression hit us and we lost all our furniture and had to separate with our children. We have four of them with us again."

Charles Minor, a father of five, whose immediate task at hand was mere survival, confessed: "Some of the children need shoes, others need clothes, and unless some good person sends us a dinner, we haven't got a thing in sight."

Well, a "good person" named Sam Stone made sure the Minor family was able to gather around a Christmas meal.

In such a way, Stone entered their lives and intersected his own with the jobless and the bankrupt of Canton. His sheltering words renewed spirits and sturdied a few weary souls trying to make their way through another day. Sam Stone reminded the downtrodden: You are not alone, someone cares. And, in the end, these words of his carried a higher value than any check he mailed. They were a gift he gave which none could see.

The *New York Times* broke the story of the suitcase on December 22, 2008 with an editorial piece written by the man who freed the case from its hiding place beneath the eaves of a cramped attic on June 24, 2008. His name was Ted Gup, Sam Stone's grandson, and the article he wrote became the second-most e-mailed story in the *New York Times*. Readers were impacted worldwide, and responses poured in from England, China, Italy, Japan, Israel, Saudi Arabia, and Brazil.

The mysterious suitcase had found its way into capable hands.

The men who wrote to B. Virdot wanted a life that included a paycheck.

"You, whoever you are," wrote Bill Gray, "I don't want charity, I want work." And from Alwyn McCort came these words: "Now, I am not asking for charity, but thought since you are interested in unfortunate people you might be able to help me get a job."

"Should I be fortunate enough to be one of the fifty or seventy-five men granted aid," wrote C. Leroy Stewart, "I request that you supply your real name so that this may be repaid with interest when the writer obtains remunerative employment."

George Carlin just wanted to be able to take his wife home for Christmas: "I could use two dollars so that my wife and I could go to her home in Alliance, but as a loan."

Ted Gup was a professor of journalism at Emerson College and had previously worked as an investigative reporter. He was also a man who understood the historical value of the documents enclosed. He further possessed the necessary skills to reconstruct the details of his grandfather's Good Samaritan gesture. With expertise and disciplined diligence, Gup tracked down over 500 descendants of the original letter-writers and included his research in his outstanding book, *A Secret Gift*.

Digital copies of the letters to B. Virdot were given to the William McKinley Presidential Library and to the Stark County Historical Society in Canton, Ohio, as well as to the Franklin D. Roosevelt Presidential Library in Hyde Park, New York.

Three anonymous donors, inspired by the story, opened a secret fund in Canton, Ohio in 2010 to assist the present-day poor of that city. (More than half of Canton's children—53.7%—live below the poverty level.)

The trio of givers, hiding their identity, deposited $5,000 each. They were patterning their plan to mirror that of Sam Stone's from nearly eighty Christmases past. Their intention was to send $100 to 150 families in hopes that B. Virdot could "live again." It was a feeling they wanted to know.

A catholic priest, a protestant minister, and a Jewish rabbi were given the task of reading the letters and assigning checks. They too worked under anonymity.

The local newspaper, where the ad originally appeared on that December day long ago, wrote an article about the 2010 efforts. The story paid tribute to the benevolent heart of Sam Stone, the fund's inspiration.

Checks then began to pour in from around the country, multiplying like loaves and fishes. Many of them were written in the amount of $100 and included notes—signed "B. Virdot"—asking that the donation be used to "help one more family." These charitable acts were an example of "each one, reach one," and $15,000 soon turned into $50,000.

As the contributions continued to accumulate, it became clear: B. Virdot was alive and well. The invented man's deeds were "like magic seeds that took root in the snow and freezing cold of Canton in that winter of 1933," observed fellow Ohioan Dr. John Giver. And a harvest was being reaped generations later.

"Perhaps the name 'Kris Kringle' is fictitious too," wrote the *Canton Repository* on December 18, 1933, "but the genuineness of the spirit of giving he represents has never been questioned." Against such wisdom, B. Virdot's existence is as sure as our own.

"Make a rule and pray to God to help you keep it, never, if possible, to lie down at night without being able to say, 'I have made one human being a little wiser, or a littler happier, or at least a little better this day.'"

Charles Kingsley

Soup kitchen, 1933

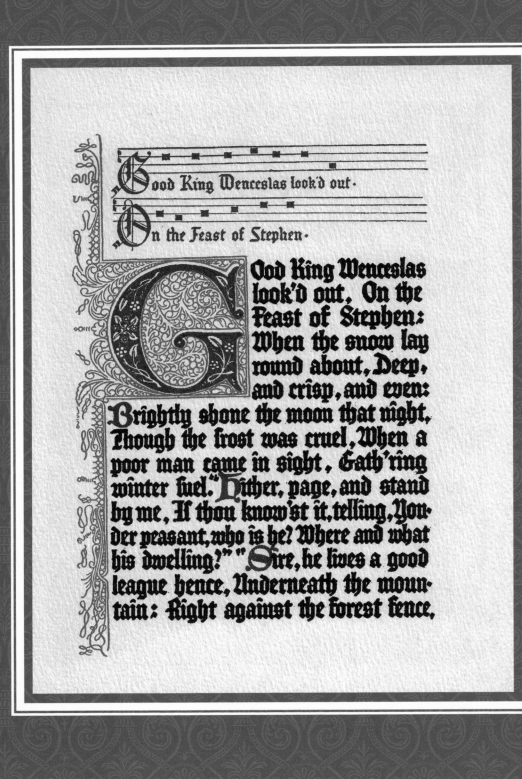

Good King Wenceslas look'd out.

On the Feast of Stephen.

God King Wenceslas look'd out, On the Feast of Stephen: When the snow lay round about, Deep, and crisp, and even: Brightly shone the moon that night, Though the frost was cruel, When a poor man came in sight, Gath'ring winter fuel. "Hither, page, and stand by me, If thou know'st it, telling, Yonder peasant, who is he? Where and what his dwelling?" "Sire, he lives a good league hence, Underneath the mountain: Right against the forest fence,

GOOD KING WENCESLAS

A thousand years have passed since "Good King Wenceslas," historical Duke of Bohemia, left his castle in the middle of a December winter storm to deliver food and fuel to a weary peasant. The years have passed, but the memory of the kindly king's gift has not.

His charitable deed lives on, immortalized in the words of the beloved Christmas carol of the same name, sung the world over each holiday season, its moral message memorized by many.

Wenceslas's face appeared on coins in the Kingdom of Bohemia for centuries thereafter, and churches were erected in his honor.

The monarch's legacy was summarized in 1119 A.D. by the medieval historian Cosmas of Prague: "He was not only a prince, but the father of all the wretched."

Image left: Johann Fust and Peter Schoeffer calligraphy print, 1457

A child, born inside the formidable stone walls of Stochov Castle in 907 A.D., was destined for the throne of Bohemia. To commemorate the royal arrival of this European prince, the infant's grandmother, Ludmila, planted an oak seedling, digging into the earth with her own hands. A thousand years later nothing remains of the castle, but the tree yet stands, as does the name of the child, Wenceslas, meaning "great glory."

As ruler, Wenceslas was famed for his philanthropy and his assistance to strangers. He became a shining light to his kingdom during its dark days of strife and unrest. Ancient artists depict Wenceslas's righteous reign in inspired images of him providing shelter to orphans, delivering wood to the poverty stricken, buying young children out of slavery, founding a hospice, and building the church of St. Vitus in Prague Castle, acts which endeared him to his people.

Wenceslas's life was formatively influenced by the Christian

GOOD KING WENCESLAS

Traditional
Harmonized by Sir John Stainer

principles of generosity endowed to him by his grandparents. His grandfather, Duke Borivoj, established the first Christian church in Bohemia and was one of the first Czech rulers to be baptized. Borivoj's son, Duke Vratislav (Wenceslas's father), also commissioned a church, St. George's at Prague Castle, while working tirelessly to strengthen Christianity throughout the land.

Prague Castle, erected by Wenceslas's grandfather, was the chosen residence of three generations—Wenceslas, his father, and his grandfather—during each of their respective reigns. Although rebuilt several times on the same site during the years following its original construction in the ninth century, the castle remains the central seat of power for the present Head of State and is a prestigious architectural landmark, as well as the largest castle complex in the world.

Wenceslas's remains are enshrined at St. Vitus Cathedral within the walled grounds. The ruler's date of death, September 28, is a national holiday in the Czech Republic and is celebrated as Czech Statehood Day. When Czechoslovakia became a sovereign state in 1918, the liberated people assembled around a statue of Wenceslas, located in Wenceslas Square, to bear witness to the reading of the Proclamation of Independence.

One of the oldest known Bohemian songs from the Middle Ages is dedicated to "Wenceslas the Good." Tradition holds that the carol, a fitting tribute, was composed by Bishop Vojtech in the tenth century and was sung as the national anthem for generations by noblemen and commoners alike.

It is not this ancient musical refrain, however, which carried the Bohemian's name across the map of the world, but rather the carol "Good King Wenceslas," written in the 1800s by an English clergyman, Reverend John Mason Neale. Although Neale composed nearly 300 hymns, he is remembered primarily for only three, each holding a dominant place in history: "O Come, O Come Emmanuel," "Good Christian Men, Rejoice," and "Good King Wenceslas."

Neale used a melody of antiquity, dating back seven centuries, for the Yuletide ballad and added original lyrics which told a poetic story set in the time of kings and queens. The stirring account praised the virtues of Wenceslas, a man loved by the subjects of his kingdom for his tender heart.

The carol, a favorite of many, is sung at Christmastime even though its words commemorate an event which happened on the "Feast of Stephen," held December 26 rather than December 25.

One night, as the verses recount, King Wenceslas looked out of his castle window and spotted a "yonder peasant" trying to gather wood for a fire. The king was deeply moved by this sight because snow was accumulating, "deep and crisp," and was accompanied by cutting winds. Any poor soul wandering in such an offending storm must surely have been desperate.

When a poor man came in sight,
Gath'ring winter fuel.

Good King Wenceslas

Good King Wenceslas look'd out,
On the Feast of Stephen;
When the snow lay round about,
Deep, and crisp, and even:
Brightly shone the moon that night,
Though the frost was cruel,
When a poor man came in sight,
Gath'ring winter fuel.

King Wenceslas, bronze statue

Taking pity on the impoverished man, King Wenceslas shouted for his faithful servant, a page named Podevin, to come to the window and identify the stranger.

Stanza 2:
"Hither, page, and stand by me, if thou know'st it, telling,
  Yonder peasant, who is he? Where and what his dwelling?"
"Sire, he lives a good league hence, underneath the mountain,
  Right against the forest fence by Saint Agnes's fountain."

The king now knew who the peasant was and where he lived. Quickly, he gave orders for provisions to be made ready for delivery to the poor man's dwelling. Then, into the harsh winter's night the king went forth with Podevin beside him.

Stanza 3:
"Bring me flesh, and bring me wine, bring me pine logs hither;
  Thou and I will see him dine when we bear them thither."
Page and monarch forth they went, forth they went together;
Through the rude wind's wild lament, and the bitter weather.

The storm railed against Wenceslas and Podevin as they trudged onward with labored breath. Soon, under the severity of the elements, the servant was beaten down and collapsed. Helping him to his feet again, Wenceslas assumed the lead, offering his body as a shield against the wind.

Stanza 4:
"Sire, the night is darker now, and the wind blows stronger;
  Fails my heart, I know not how; I can go no longer."
"Mark my footsteps, my good page, tread thou in them boldly.
Thou shalt find the winter's rage freezes thy blood less coldly."

Image right: King Wenceslas, painting by Jessie Marion King, 1919

GOOD·KING·WENCESLAVS

"PAGE·AND·MONARCH·FORTH·THEY·WENT
FORTH·THEY·WENT·TOGETHER"

What happened next is recorded as the Miracle of Wenceslas. Stepping behind the king, the weakened page saw a light shining forth from the monarch's body. Blades of grass sprung up from beneath the king's footprints, melting the snow. The love and warmth of his generous heart was radiating around him, and both men were now engulfed in a protective barrier of light as they traveled the remaining distance to the other side of the mountain to deliver the gifts they came bearing—food, wine, logs, and love.

Stanza 5:
In his master's steps he trod, where the snow lay dinted;
Heat was in the very sod, which the saint had printed.
Therefore, Christian men, be sure, wealth or rank possessing;
Ye who now will bless the poor, shall yourselves find blessing.

I suppose it could be said that the carol bearing Wenceslas's name has nothing to do with Christmas, or I suppose it could be said that it has everything to do with Christmas. Why? Because the kind king's mission was an embodiment of the Christian message which urges each of us to "feed the hungry, clothe the naked, welcome the stranger, and serve one another in love," and, in so doing, learn the truth of the words "it is more blessed to give than it is to receive."

The carol hits the soft spot in my heart every year because I too once looked upon a starving man in the snow at Christmas, but unlike the peasant in King Wenceslas's story, the man I speak of did not live happily ever after. Why? Because everyone was too busy celebrating Christmas for all of the wrong reasons.

I was a young woman at the time, not even twenty years old. A few friends and I decided to see a live performance of *A Christmas Carol* at the Pabst Theater in Milwaukee, Wisconsin. We heard about the elegant theater and couldn't wait to attend. The experience was

Johann Fust and Peter Schoeffer calligraphy print, 1457

everything we thought it would be, and more. Then we left, and that is when I saw him. A ragged man was lying against a brick building on the frozen ground like a bag of garbage. We all saw him, even those who pretended not to.

Then I watched as everyone walked right past him. In shoes that

Did you know…?

Wenceslas's remains are enshrined at Prague Castle in St. Vitus Cathedral. A mere wall separates the grave of Wenceslas from that of his faithful servant, Podevin.

Wenceslas's helmet, armor, iron shirt, and sword are held in the castle treasury. The sword was used for knighting ceremonies centuries after his death.

The "Crown of Wenceslas," a magnificent relic covered in emeralds, pearls, egg-sized sapphires, and rubies as large as a fist, can be seen at Prague Castle. Charles IV commissioned the crown for his coronation in the 1300s and dedicated it to the memory of Wenceslas. He then directed that the crown, which rested upon the skull of Wenceslas, be worn at all coronations of Czech kings.

Prague was the third most prominent city in all of Europe in the 1300s, after Rome and Constantinople. It is still recognized today as one of Europe's most beautiful.

Although Wenceslas was only a duke during his lifetime, Holy Roman Emperor Otto I posthumously conferred on him the regal dignity and title of king.

Image left: Prague Castle, wood engraving, 1493

matched dresses, holding purses that matched shoes, the crowd kept right on going.

A stranger beside me mumbled, "Why doesn't the city do something to expand those overflowing shelters so we don't have to look at that?"

The homeless man annoyed the beautiful woman. To her, he was not a him, he was a "that." It was a cold word, an icy word—cold, like the night.

Life is tough for too many people in this world, people who have to swallow hard as they wait for the next blow to hit them, and it does. Where is the help these people hope for? It's inside of you, and inside of me.

I wish I could go back to help that nameless man I saw lying in the darkness and do something kind and good for him. If I could return, I would, but all the wishing in the world cannot take me to that place. The wish cannot be granted.

On that night long ago, I was afraid. I had never before witnessed such suffering, or traveled to the city at dark without my parents, or met someone who didn't have a porch light waiting at day's end. I should have said something, or did something, but I didn't, regrettably.

I never found the homeless man's face again, but neither have I forgotten it.

Life is fleeting, and its moments for us to be miracles pass quickly; then they are gone forever.

Knowing this, let us go forth—"forth they went together"—and search for the face of need. It is everywhere. It is on the hungry, and it is on the heartbroken.

Then, when we find it, let us ask ourselves if we will be an answer to this person's prayer. Will we be their miracle?

The strength of humanity lies in the willingness for each of us to leave the walls of our own lives and connect with the lives of others in the spirit of "goodwill toward men."

Lead on.

The spirit of Christmas is found in the singing,
in the bright Christmas trees and the bells that are ringing.
The spirit is found in the lights everywhere,
but the meaning is found in the love people share.

Amish Proverb

Old Chelsea mansion house

1855 drawing by Mary Moore Ogden, daughter of Clement C. Moore

The above image appeared on the first interior page of a booklet produced by Mary Moore Ogden as a Christmas gift for her husband. The poem, written in calligraphy, was complimented by visual renderings of her father's words, the first known color illustrations of the poem.

"'Twas the Night Before Christmas"

On a 94-acre New York countryside estate named Chelsea, in a lovely mansion overlooking the Hudson River, Clement C. Moore picked up a goose's feather, dipped it in ink, and began to pen "the most beloved and memorized poem in the entire English language," "A Visit from St. Nicholas," better known by the poem's first line, "'Twas the Night Before Christmas."

It was Christmas Eve afternoon 1822, and the enchanted verses were written as a gift for Moore's six children, youngsters barely the height of their father's knee.

Candles flickered behind the shuttered windows of the stately mansion later that evening, and plumes of smoke, retreating skyward, rose from the many chimneys crowning Chelsea's rooftop as the "Poet of Christmas Eve" sat fireside, in the same home where he had spent his own childhood, and read the verses for the first time, capturing the imaginations of the little ones gathered around him.

The words gifted to the Moore children on that distant Christmas Eve became a gift to all the world's children ever after.

Clement Clarke Moore, author of "'Twas the Night Before Christmas," the most widely read and recited poem in all of children's literature, was the only child of the distinguished Benjamin Moore and his wife, Charity Clarke, a woman whose family tree included English royals. At his birth in 1779, Clement was christened with a name extending honor to both sides of his ancestry.

As a child and young adult, Clement's impressive intellect was nurtured in Chelsea's scholarly household. He became a brilliant student and an accomplished musician, playing both organ and violin. He was fluent in six languages—English, French, Greek, Hebrew, Latin, and Italian—as well as a gifted architect. His advancement in academic endeavors was so remarkable that by the age of nineteen he graduated from New York's Columbia College (today Columbia University), placing first in his class, a feat accomplished by his

Mr. and Mrs. Clement C. Moore

Clement C. Moore did not marry until he was thirty-four years old. It was then that he met the beautiful Catherine Elizabeth Taylor, a gracious, intelligent young woman with a "poetic soul" who captivated his heart. Moore was so utterly smitten with her loveliness that he was unable to gather his thoughts. In a letter addressed to his mother, dated October 16, 1813, Moore shared details of his happiness: "Catherine and I ramble about in the country and talk all manner of nonsense. I cut her name upon the trees, and try, without success, to make verses."

They were married one month later on November 20, 1813.

The Moore household was blessed with nine children (three sons and six daughters): Margaret, Charity, Benjamin, Mary, Clement Jr., Emily, William, Catherine, and Maria Theresa. The three youngest of the brood were not yet born in 1822 when their father gave his first reading of his rhythmic holiday verses.

Although Catherine was only nineteen years old when she became Mrs. Moore, she preceded her husband in death by many years. He lived to the age of eighty-four, and she to only thirty-six. Moore was "inconsolable" at the passing of his bride. He never remarried.

Moore's mother, who lived with the family, helped her son raise the children until her death in 1838 at the age of ninety-one. Chelsea estate had been her home for eighty-eight years, nearly the whole of her life.

1732 1799

Washington
crossing the
Deleware.

Christmas Day, 1776
Vintage postcard

George Washington's brave act of crossing the Delaware River on Christmas Day with his Continental Army to face enemy British troops during the Revolutionary War (1775-1783) was a turning point in our country's grasp for freedom.

Sometime during the following year, General Washington paid a visit to Moore's Chelsea mansion. He rode out to the homestead on his famous white horse to offer apologies to the Moore family for the conduct of soldiers who overran their property during a subsequent scrimmage.

The Chelsea estate was next offended by British soldiers who unintentionally shot a cannonball through a wall in the home.

highly educated father before him at the exact same age. Benjamin Moore, an ordained protestant deacon, priest, and New York Bishop of the Episcopalian faith, went on to serve as president of Columbia.

Both the elder and younger Moore held masters and doctoral degrees.

A notable event in Bishop Benjamin Moore's career was his assistance in officiating at the presidential inauguration of George Washington.

Clement Moore was deeply influenced by his father's spiritual achievements and chose to serve in a teaching capacity at the General Theological Seminary in New York where he was a professor of Greek and Oriental literature, as well as a professor of divinity and Biblical learning. His teaching career followed an authorship of the first Hebrew dictionary in the United States, *A Compendious Lexicon of the Hebrew Language*, an exhaustive feat.

The General Theological Seminary was built on land donated by Clement Moore. The parcel, formerly the family's apple orchard, covered an entire city block and was gifted under the condition that the building constructed be used to educate and ordain ministers. Additional land from the Moore estate was donated to the Episcopal Church of St. Peter, a beautiful cathedral built a mere block from the seminary shortly thereafter. Both institutions credit Moore as a founding father, and both are still serving in the capacity of his vision nearly two hundred years later on Manhattan's West Side.

Although the stately Chelsea mansion no longer exists, nor the wooded hill it stood upon—a crest once covered with gardens, orchards, oaks, weeping willows, and a walnut grove—the neighborhood where the homestead was located is still referred to as the "Chelsea" section of New York City, an area presently bordered by Nineteenth to Twenty-fourth Streets, and Eighth to Tenth Avenues.

Mary Moore Sherman, granddaughter of Clement Moore, included her thoughts on Old Chelsea in her 1906 book of recollections:

I wonder if any of the numerous people who pass the crowd of laborers along the riverfront in the neighborhood of West Twenty-third Street, and see the great works now in progress there—the stone piers where steamers that hold a town full of folk will find accommodation, the ferry-houses where ever-increasing throngs hurry to and from the city—I wonder if any of the passers gives a thought to the peaceful country place whose green lawns sloped down to the river so short a time ago, and under whose stately trees there lived little more than half a century since the genial gentleman, scholar, poet, and musician, Clement C. Moore, the author of "'Twas the Night Before Christmas."

In the spacious comfortable house that was almost hidden in its foliage from outsiders, surrounded by a large family, he dwelt for years, extending hospitality to many of the distinguished strangers who visited New York. The city, however, gradually encroached on the quiet country place, and the house was finally pulled down to give way to the demands of the times.

A versatile man was Mr. Moore, being a professor in the General Theological Seminary, which he enriched with a princely fortune, and organist in St. Peter's Church, which he contributed largely to erect, whose graystone walls and towers remain unchanged. In his idle moments he played skillfully on his violin, and composed for his children poems, of which one, at least, touched the heartcords of the children of the world. Even now, from all the distant corners of the globe, wherever the English-speaking race has penetrated, their joyful voices lisp forth the dearly-loved verses. And when, after calling up the chimney to their faithful friend not to forget this or that much longed-for present, they go to their little beds, are not their curly heads full of dreams all night of reindeer on the roof, and are they not certain they heard St. Nicholas whistling, and shouting, and calling them by name? And the magician who wrought for them these visions was Clement C. Moore, the last occupant of the lovely country place named Chelsea.

Thomas Nast illustration, 1876

Thomas Nast illustration, 1881

He died in July, 1863, in the eighty-fourth year of his age. He was universally mourned, for both old and young loved the gentle, courteous, childlike scholar. May his memory be kept green in their hearts. Dearly did he love children, and it is only right that he, as well as his verses, should live in their memories.

Perhaps some cold winter's day, when the little ones go out just after a snowstorm to build their snow castles and snowmen, some of the more thoughtful ones may pause for a moment before beginning their work and, surveying the lovely scene, may think of these lines, written by my grandfather:

> *Come, children dear, and look around—*
> *Behold how soft and light*
> *The silent snow has clad the ground*
> *In robes of purest white.*
>
> *The trees seem decked by fairy hands,*
> *Nor need their native green;*
> *And every breeze appears to stand,*
> *All hushed to view the scene.*

Mary Moore Sherman's hope for her grandfather's memory to be "kept green" was fulfilled. He was eulogized at his funeral with the words "large-minded and always a learner," and the Reverend Dr. Tuttle fittingly spoke of the quiet man as "that accomplished scholar, Christian gentleman, and noble benefactor to literature and theology."

Perhaps the most ironic words spoken were these: "He was content to be overlooked by the world." But history, as we well know, was unwilling to let Clement Moore's accomplishments fade from view. In particular, it would be his composition of "the little poem," as he came to refer to it, which would be the defining merry masterpiece of his life, despite the countless intellectually stimulating lectures the knowledge-seeker prepared while sitting at the same desk in his study where he wrote: "He had a broad face and a little round belly, that shook when he laughed like a bowl full of jelly."

The poet's memory is preserved today in New York City's oldest, continuous Christmas tradition which takes place, surprisingly, in a cemetery. For a hundred years, without interruption, children of all ages, from eight to eighty-eight, have paid homage to Moore's wondrous words, and to his contribution to the blessed eve, by marching to his final resting place and reverently placing a wreath of fresh greenery upon the family's gravestone. This annual honoring began on Christmas Day 1911.

The memorial begins at the nearby Church of the Intercession where the author's celebrated lines of verse are narrated. Those gathered then proceed down the hillside to "the revered spot" in

Did you know...?

Two parks in New York City bear Clement Clarke Moore's name:

Clement Clarke Moore Park is located at the corner of Twenty-second Street and Tenth Avenue on land purchased by Moore's maternal grandfather, Captain Thomas Clarke, in 1750.

Clement Clarke Moore Homestead is located in Newtown, Queens, on land purchased by Moore's paternal great-great grandfather, Captain Samuel Moore, in 1652.

Clement Clarke Moore Candlelight Commemoration

The Children's Pilgrimage

An Annual Christmas Tradition in New York City

Trinity Church Cemetery, 1930

The above illustration was included in the book *A Visit of St. Nicholas*, published by McLoughlin Brothers in 1862. The artist inadvertently painted ten reindeer for the centerfold image instead of eight. (He correctly portrayed Santa's sleigh with eight reindeer on the other pages of the publication.)

Now Dasher! Now Dancer! Now Prancer and Vixen!
On Comet! On Cupid! On Donner and Blitzen!
To the top of the porch! To the top of the wall!
Now dash away! Dash away! Dash away all!

Trinity Church Cemetery on foot, carrying lit lanterns. The procession ends with carol singing in the graveyard, and a candlelight ceremony expressing gratitude for the author, whose memory today rests almost solely on the timeless appeal of the whimsical words he wove together in his immortal Yuletide ballad. From the poem's first line to its last, Moore invited his readers to enter the magical kingdom of Christmas, accessible through imagination only. He painted fanciful visions across the minds of his readers and, in so doing, earned himself a place on bookshelves—and hearts—around the world.

"Unknowingly," wrote the poet's biographer, Samuel Patterson, "Clement C. Moore built his own memorial more enduring than brass or marble. On the hearts of little children, his name is inscribed forever."

Image right: Four copies of Clement C. Moore's poem, written in the author's own handwriting, are known to exist. A copy held by the New York Historical Society appears on the following pages.

Two additional copies are held in public archives at the Strong Museum in Rochester, New York, and the Henry E. Huntington Library in San Marino, California. Only one copy penned by Moore is in private hands. It was recently sold by the Heritage Auction Galleries to an unnamed collector living in Manhattan for $280,000.00.

'Twas the night before Christmas, when all through
    the house
Not a creature was stirring, not even a mouse;
The stockings were hung by the chimney with care,
In hopes that St. Nicholas soon would be there;
The children were nestled all snug in their beds,
While visions of sugar-plums danced in their heads;
And Mamma in her 'kerchief, and I in my cap,
Had just settled our brains for a long winter's nap;
When out on the lawn there arose such a clatter,
I sprang from the bed to see what what was the matter.
Away to the window I flew like a flash,
Tore open the shutters and threw up the sash.
The moon, on the breast of the new-fallen snow,
Gave the lustre of mid-day to objects below,
When, what to my wondering eyes should appear,
But a miniature sleigh, and eight tiny rein-deer,
With a little old driver, so lively and quick,
I knew in a moment it must be St. Nick.
More rapid than eagles his coursers they came,
And he whistled, and shouted, and called them by name;

"Now, <u>Dasher</u>! now, <u>Dancer</u>! now, <u>Prancer</u> and <u>Vixen</u>!
On, <u>Comet</u>! on, <u>Cupid</u>! on, <u>Donder</u> and <u>Blitzen</u>!
To the top of the porch! to the top of the wall!
Now dash away! dash away! dash away all!"
As dry leaves that before the wild hurricane fly,
When they meet with an obstacle, mount to the sky;
So up to the house-top the coursers they flew,
With the sleigh full of Toys, and St. Nicholas too.
And then, in a twinkling, I heard on the roof
The prancing and pawing of each little hoof —
As I drew in my head, and was turning around,
Down the chimney St. Nicholas came with a bound.
He was dressed all in fur, from his head to his foot,
And his clothes were all tarnished with ashes and soot;
A bundle of Toys he had flung on his back,
And he look'd like a pedlar just opening his pack.
His eyes — how they twinkled! his dimples how merry!
His cheeks were like roses, his nose like a cherry!
His droll little mouth was drawn up like a bow
And the beard of his chin was as white as the snow;
The stump of a pipe he held tight in his teeth,

And the smoke it encircled his head like a wreath;
He had a broad face and a little round belly
That shook, when he laughed, like a bowl full of jelly.
He was chubby and plump, a right jolly old elf,
And I laughed, when I saw him, in spite of myself;
A wink of his eye and a twist of his head,
Soon gave me to know I had nothing to dread;

He spoke not a word, but went straight to his work,
And fill'd all the stockings; then turned with a jerk,
And laying his finger aside of his nose,
And giving a nod, up the chimney he rose;
He sprang to his sleigh, to his team gave a whistle,
And away they all flew like the down of a thistle.
But I heard him exclaim, ere he drove out of sight,
"<u>Happy Christmas to all, and to all a good night.</u>"

Clement C. Moore,
1862, March 13th originally written
many years ago.

"The story of the Christmas Tree Ship will ever remain as green as the trees she carried."

Milwaukee Sentinel

THE CHRISTMAS TREE SHIP

At the center of the Christmas Tree Ship story beats the heart of Captain Herman Schuenemann, a man whose eyes were blue like the sea he loved.

This "gallant skipper" delivered evergreens on the shores of Lake Michigan in the late 1800s and early 1900s, gifting many of the trees to underprivileged families, churches, and orphanages during that time.

After the captain's passing, his kind deeds lived on, especially in the hearts and minds of those who waited at the docks in Chicago for the sight of sails and the smell of pine come November.

Chicago memorialized Captain Schuenemann in 1913 by erecting the city's first municipal Christmas tree. The towering evergreen, dedicated to him, paid tribute to all the captain had done to bring Christmas to the city.

The tree was lit, fittingly, on Christmas Eve afternoon as a "sea of humanity" looked on. Over 100,000 people gathered to honor the captain's story, a story which exemplified the best of humanity—generosity, heroism, steadfastness, and the importance of family.

The Schuenemann legacy intertwines courage, faith, and a commitment to those we love. The very idea of the Christmas tree—symbol of everlasting life and everlasting hope— being at the story's center, encompasses who the Schuenemanns were, and what they believed.

From one generation to the next, the captain's memory has held its place in history as one of the "greatest of the Great Lakes." His deeds have been kept alive by poets and painters, and by songwriters and storytellers. These are the guardians who continue to breathe life into the captain's life long gone.

The year was 1912, and the month was November. Autumn had fallen asleep in northern Michigan, and winter was just rising. It would rise on the land first, and then move into the waters, freezing them solid.

There was still a little time for Captain Schuenemann to make his last sail of the season, but he needed to hurry if he didn't want to meet Old Man Winter out on the waters, the worst possible place. He knew this, and was doing just that—hurrying, hurrying. The winds were telling him, and the waves also, "Hurry, Captain, hurry." These were the voices whispering around him in those moments at the break of dawn. He listened.

Then the captain reached a decision: "We sail." He would delay no further. Thick ropes anchoring the wooden ship to the shore began to be untied.

Captain Schuenemann was on his way to Chicago with a load of freshly cut Christmas trees, a majestic cargo of Yuletide cheer. Five

Hauling evergreens from the Christmas Tree Ship downtown Chicago, 1904

They're the people you must see if you want a Christmas tree!
With every tree, they give a smile!
Vintage advertisement for Schuenemann trees

"Sailing Into Eternity," painting by Eric Forsberg

"I guess the kids are gladdest of anybody to see us come pulling into the river every December," said Captain Schuenemann. "There's generally a crowd of them on the rail of the bridge when it swings open for us, and they wave their hands and cheer, and we cheer back. Some of them think we are actually coming from the North Pole."

Chicago Inter-Ocean newspaper
December 7, 1909

thousand evergreens filled the ship's belly, and another five hundred, heaped high, were tied to its decks. Pine scented the harbor and those gathered there breathed in deeply this first fragrance of Christmas.

The last tree brought aboard, a spruce, was then fastened to the tip of the top of the tallest of the three sails, as was the particular tradition of this particular ship. From there, a place of honor, it adorned both the vessel and its holiday load, like a star atop a tree, but instead, a tree atop a ship, a crown of sorts, the identifying mark of the Christmas Tree Ship.

Every Christmas, the captain and his sailing vessel made this voyage together, down to the Clark Street Bridge in Chicago, just off Michigan Avenue. Captain Schuenemann waited the whole long year for this journey, his favorite of all. He loved Christmas, and loved delivering his trees to the docks, as he had done since 1887, where he sold them right off his ship for as little as a dime or as much as a whole dollar. And what a sight his ship was with wreaths hung from every rail!

To the folks in Chicago who awaited its annual arrival, the ship had become the ultimate symbol of Christmas, and its captain, a hero. He was a man who "always had a kind word or friendly wave to spare," and his generosity in giving free trees away to churches, orphanages, schoolrooms, and to any family who otherwise wouldn't have been able to afford one, gave cause for him to acquire an affectionate nickname: Captain Santa. Hearing it made the ruddy-faced skipper smile, especially when spoken by the children. They'd be waiting for him on the docks when he approached the harbor, edging his ship in, shores parting before it. "Captain Santa's here! Captain Santa!" they'd shout.

Vincent Starrett, a Chicago newspaper journalist who personally knew Captain Schuenemann in the early 1900s, reported: "The Christmas season didn't really arrive in Chicago until the Christmas

Chicago Daily News, 1917

Captain Schuenemann's wife, Barbara, would weave boughs and wreaths along with their three daughters. Elsie is pictured next to her mother in the lower photo, and the twins, Pearlie and Hazel, appear in the upper photo.

Tree Ship tied up at the Clark Street Bridge." And according to the *Chicago Tribune*, Captain Herman and his boat became "as much a part of Chicago's Christmas as Santa Claus."

Chicago's St. Paul's Church included the following entry in their 1906 December newsletter: "Captain Schuenemann, the old mariner, who gets within an ace of being shipwrecked every year when he sails away to Santa Claus's Land to get a big ship full of Christmas trees, what did he do? Well, he sent a wagonload of trees, wreaths, and festoons to the church, parsonage, and orphanage. And when a meek little man went down and asked for the bill, Captain Schuenemann roared down Clark Street like a foghorn: 'Blow the bill!' So that's what became of *that* bill, it was blowed."

In 1912, the captain had a towering tree for the congregation of St. Paul's on his ship. Soon, he'd be delivering it, and soon he'd be back home again.

That is what he told his wife as she stood there on the pier beside him. She wanted to know about the ship's return, and his also. She always did. When the waters separated them, her heart from his, his from hers, she wondered when he would be home. And he would tell her the same answer each time he left, "Soon. I'll be home soon." It was an unchanging response to her unchanging question, yet still she asked, and still he answered.

Then dawn broke forth into day on that November morning, lingering for just a moment in shades of crimson, lingering, this dawn, like the captain's dear wife on the planks of a paintless pier where she waved goodbye, waving with the waters, "Goodbye, Captain, goodbye."

The great ship was set in motion, an aging schooner, weathered and weary, in the twilight of its sailing days. With Chicago somewhere before them, and Thompson's Landing in Michigan's Upper Peninsula now behind, the captain's hands grabbed hold of

A Memory of Chicago's Christmas Tree Ship

Jimmy O'Malley remembered his family purchasing an evergreen from the Christmas Ship, as well as having received a free tree, gifted to the family by the ship's generous-hearted captain, when poverty prevented the O'Malleys from paying.

Born in 1894 to Irish immigrants, Jimmy was the oldest of nine children. He recalled "carrying a dime," clutched in his little hand, down to the tree-laden ship where he and his brothers and sisters would climb aboard.

"The arrival of Skipper Schuenemann's schooner generated so much excitement that nothing else in the world mattered when the Christmas Ship came in," he told his children and grandchildren. "The schooner was greeted with such exuberance you could hear shouts in the street, heralding the holiday news, as the vessel approached."

"If my grandfather's family had not received a free tree," remembered Jean Kopecky, granddaughter of Jimmy O'Malley, "they would not have had any tree during several years when the family fell on particularly hard times. Every penny was precious to the O'Malleys. There was hardly enough money for food, and certainly no money for a Christmas tree."

She told how her grandfather looked forward to the arrival of the Christmas Ship as the most "highly anticipated" moment of his holiday.

"Wearing shoes that buttoned up to his ankles—even with holes in—and faded, hand-me-down clothes, my grandfather headed to the docks with his brothers and sisters to see the captain," she said. "Regardless of how cold it was, or if someone only had one mitten, nothing else in the world mattered when the Christmas Ship sailed in."

The O'Malley kids' heights went down like steps, one right after the other, and when they carried their Christmas tree home on their shoulders, it looked like a giant bug with nine sets of legs beneath it walking along the cobblestone streets. Jimmy, the oldest, and tallest, would carry the heaviest end of the tree, gripping the trunk where the branches were most full. His youngest sibling, on the opposite end, would reach up high and hold the tip.

A century of Christmases have gone by since the "evergreen bug" paraded along Chicago's streets, past gaslight lanterns decorated with Schuenemann wreaths, yet the smiles born from Captain Schuenemann's many kindnesses are still lighting up the faces of grandchildren and great-grandchildren who have become the living repositories of their ancestors' oral history.

"Always, I remember my grandpa being anxious for Christmas," remembered another O'Malley grandchild, "but it was not the Christmases of the present that he longed for. He was anxious to remember the Christmases of the past—*long past*."

Grandpa O'Malley continued to hold dear "the warmth" of his childhood days when he stood on the snow-dusted decks of the Christmas Ship with holes in his shoes.

Christmas Tree Ship, 1908, in the Chicago harbor

the wooden wheel with its spokes and spines that would navigate his vessel through unseen passageways in the open waters spreading themselves before him.

To his crew waiting on deck, Captain Schuenemann called out, "Unleash the sails! Raise 'em high!" And they did.

Then the captain saw it. It was the one sight he loved more than any other when he was out to sea, the sight of seemingly being able to see forever across endless waters and an endless horizon.

Somewhere out there Chicago lay. The captain knew it, but for now, it appeared not to be so. For now, it looked as if he and his ship could sail on forever into infinity. He embraced the sight with his arms spread wide across the width of the wheel he worked before him. *Sail on, Captain, sail on.*

Yes, if there was a sight more beautiful than the horizon, the captain knew not what it was. And he had seen many, especially out here, a place where moonbeams gathered at midnight to dance on a watery floor beneath lanterns hung high in the sky. And he would dance with them, this captain, shuffling his feet on the deck to music he alone could hear—gulls singing lullabies along the shoreline and foghorns calling out in deep-throated voices.

Then slumber would beckon to him, and he would sleep in Life's arms as it rocked him back and forth, back and forth. In the great rocking chair of the waters, the captain would be rocked to a rhythm of heartbeats, the water's and his own. Tide in, tide out. Breath in, breath out. *Sleep now, Captain, sleep.*

But on the morning of November 23, 1912, sleep was the furthest thing from the captain's mind. He was awake, wide-eyed awake, acutely aware of the signs around him.

A storm was poised and ready to strike. Ominous clouds hung low on the horizon. Despite this, Captain Schuenemann believed that if he hurried, he could get his ship ahead of the storm.

Schooners departing from Kewaunee, Wisconsin

Old Man Winter was challenging the captain to a race down the lake. One of them would reach Chicago by the following day, the other not at all.

Captain Schuenemann knew the risks of being in the middle of the lake when the mood of the waters turned ugly, and he knew, as well as anyone could have, the perils of sailing in November—the most treacherous month of the year, a month when "angry storms" and "screaming blizzards" could be unleashed in a moment. After all, he had been delivering his trees for nearly a quarter of a century

"Moonlight Pass," painting by Eric Forsberg

by this time.

Most captains refused to sail in this feared month when weather could deteriorate quickly, and they saw to it that their vessels were off the Great Lakes by the end of October, but this was not an option a Christmas tree merchant had the luxury of exercising.

From where he stood at the helm of his ship, Captain Schuenemann turned around, again and again, as he looked over his shoulder, watching the gray sky behind him darken. This was no passing glance he gave the sky and its warning, but a fixed stare, worry creasing itself deeply into his brow. This changing sky meant something, and the changing current that pulled itself around him did, too. They were silent sirens telling him, "Run, Captain, run." Winter had awoken, and it was coming for him.

Winds, whipping wild out of the west, rose higher and higher as temperatures fell lower and lower. It was a deadly combination. Towering waves crashed over breaker walls along shorelines just past and gusts increased in fury, hitting hurricane velocities. Limbs were torn from trees. If Captain Schuenemann had any question about his ability to navigate his vessel safely through the surging seas, his question would be answered before the sun set on a single day more.

Rains, falling steadily, turned to whirling, swirling snow, decreasing visibility. Winds intensified and amplified their howl. The storm pounded faster and louder as it broke the hypnotic rhythm of the waves. Lake Michigan soon started to convulse and heave like an earthquake. Massive walls of water were being thrown at the ship, slamming it with stunning force. The helpless crew was now exposed to the full sweep of the gale. Ice froze to beards and brows, numbing sailors to the bone. Mounting waves climbed aboard the distressed ship, invading it, penetrating every nook and cranny, sinking it lower into the waters.

Through these heavy seas the captain ran. It was his only choice. He couldn't turn back, it was too late for that. His stricken ship was on a collision course with death. Winter was chasing Captain Schuenemann down in the most ferocious way, closing in on him from all points of the compass in the form of a mid-lateral cyclone. This was the term weathermen later used to explain what happened out there on the waters when the sky turned black and the world turned white, and Winter caught the captain.

A crew of rescue workers on duty at the United States Life Saving Station (a predecessor organization of our modern-day Coast Guard) in Kewaunee, Wisconsin picked up the captain's distress signal and radioed south to the Two Rivers Life Saving Station, asking that a crew attempt an intercept of the ship.

It was 3:10 p.m. Sunset was nearing, and the last rays of daylight were fast falling as these men labored into the surf and entered the chaotic sea. Each rescue worker who left that afternoon forged forward with the full knowledge of the price he was called to pay.

Photos can show us these men—men of steady shoulders and steady hands, of steady hearts and steady eyes—but they cannot show us the courage behind those eyes. Photos fail to capture their spirits, or their willingness to risk saving others at the cost of losing themselves. These men of unmatched bravery vowed to honor the Life Saving Station code: "We must go out, but we do not have to come back in." Every time the door closed behind them, their return was uncertain.

All over the Great Lakes, others were fighting valiant battles with the weather as "unabated fury" was hurled at multiple ill-fated vessels.

Through the dusk of the night the rescuers searched, plowing their way through confused waters churning at the will of the wind. These "storm warriors" knew the supreme value of every second,

Life Saving Station crew, 1912
Two Rivers, Wisconsin

and they understood what needed to be done—and when—as it concerned the demands upon them to pull sailors back from death's door where they hung in the balance between this world and the next. Shaking and shivering, soaked through and through, the crew looked long and hard for the doomed schooner while time ticked down. Once, they came close enough—within an eighth of a mile— to catch sight of the battered vessel coated in ice. A blinding squall of white then passed between the two, eliminating all visibility with its heavy curtain of snow. When it passed, the Christmas Tree Ship had vanished.

The rescue party did its utmost to reach the ship, but Winter reached it first, bearing down upon the stricken vessel with the full force of its weight. The crippled Christmas Tree Ship—creaking and groaning in its death struggle—was unable to sustain itself above the waters any longer. The moment of surrender arrived, and the intruding seas, pouring in, prevailed.

The gale continued to wail in the hours that followed November 23, 1912, and the skies shed their tears. These were stomach-churning days of endless pacing for family members who endured the slowness of time as they waited—morning until evening, evening until morn—for a reassuring word of their loved ones. Despite hopeful reports scattered in between alternating headlines which declared that the ship was "safe" and then "lost," and then "safe" again, hope was not to last.

Barbara Schuenemann, a person of deep faith, was praying for the life of her husband. She longed to see him step safely through the door, but hers was a prayer that could not be answered. The life she wished spared had already ended.

The only witnesses to the ship's final demise were the silent stars, the speechless moon, and the winds which howled on in their strange tongue none could understand. The secret of the Christmas Tree Ship was held tight, and its mystery lingered.

Two weeks and six days later, fishermen came across a corked bottle floating in waters near Sheboygan, Wisconsin. Within, on a torn sheet of paper ripped from Captain Schuenemann's own log, was written his farewell address: "Everybody, goodbye. I guess we are thru. Leaking badly. God help us. Signed: Herman Schuenemann."

Newspapers broke the story, including the headline printed in the Friday, December 13, 1912 issue of the *Chicago American*: Lost Ship's Story Told in a Bottle.

It had taken two weeks and six days to find the bottle, but another twelve years would pass before the captain's wallet washed ashore. The pocketbook, burgundy in color, was found in 1924 by a fishing captain and a lighthouse keeper near the very spot where the ship was last sighted.

Finding the wallet of Captain Santa was quite remarkable, but what was even more amazing was that the skipper of the fishing boat, Captain Norman Allie, had named his vessel the *Reindeer*.

Identification of the wallet, which was later turned over to the Schuenemann family, was easily made because the pocketbook had been wrapped in oilskin, a type of waterproof sailor's packing, and everything within was perfectly preserved. According to the *Manistique Pioneer-Tribune* of April 17, 1924, Schuenemann's personal business card was enclosed, as well as expense receipts and newspaper clippings. (Captain Schuenemann would cut stories out of the newspapers that told of his famed Christmas voyages each year. He then carried them around with him in his wallet. The articles, clipped from penny publications, were still readable when the pocketbook was found.)

Tell-tale evidence and debris continued to surface for decades— Christmas trees, a wooden trunk, and even the ship's 400-pound captain's wheel which had been ripped from the vessel. For the ship itself, though, fifty-nine years would pass before a scuba diver came across the submerged wreckage, undisturbed on the floor of Lake Michigan in darkened depths. He discovered the wreck quite by accident while searching for another sunken vessel off the coast

"The loss of no vessel on the Great Lakes aroused more sympathy than that of the Rouse Simmons, *known as the Christmas Tree Ship."*
Sturgeon Bay Advocate newspaper
August 26, 1927

of Two Rivers, Wisconsin in 1971.

There she was, the Christmas Tree Ship, intact and sitting upright on the lake's bottom. All doubt as to the fate of the vessel was put to rest. The diver recognized the legendary ship immediately, its trees still fastened to its deck, secured there, just as they had been that fateful day long ago, preserved in the frigid waters. This unshovelled grave of the captain had been marked by a tree, as if a grave upon the land, marked by a spruce, fastened to the tip of the top of the tallest of three sails way back when.

And so it was, that such a tree as this was fastened to a sail on another old, wooden ship being loaded with evergreens the following November of 1913 at Thompson's Landing. This voyage had been chartered by a woman of remarkable courage who stood on the planks of the same paintless pier where she had stood a year earlier, almost to the very day. Her name was Barbara, the captain's beloved wife, and under her watchful eye evergreens were going aboard this ship until it was time for her to begin her journey. And then she did.

Stepping off the pier and onto this vessel named *Fearless*, she and her precious cargo of white pine and balsam and fir were bound for Chicago where the city was waiting. They had heard, you see, that Mrs. Santa was on her way.

When her schooner sailed in, the people of Chicago were gathered on the docks just off of Michigan Avenue to welcome the captain's darling. They came by carriage, and they came by sleigh, and they came on foot, whole families hand-in-hand, to buy an evergreen from this noble woman who chose to stand in the gap between the past and the present and become heir to the tradition that was a part of their holiday and a part of their hearts.

For the next twenty Christmases, Mrs. Herman Schuenemann could be found at the accustomed place to honor her husband's

Barbara Schuenemann, 1913

memory and his love of the Christ of Christmas, the everlasting hope he held fast to for all of his days like a great wheel navigating him onward.

The *Chicago Daily News* interviewed Mrs. Schuenemann on November 28, 1913 after she returned to Chicago, and she had this to say: "It was splendid up there in the big woods. I was there for eight weeks and it seemed like one long holiday for me. Perhaps it was because I felt that somehow my husband was there with me. That's where he would have been had he been alive, and I felt somehow he was there anyway. And the smell of the pines was good, and the clear, starry nights, and the sound of the chopping all day long. I shall never miss it. Every year I shall go to the northwoods, and after I am gone, there will be others to carry on the work."

Barbara had breathed the air her husband would have breathed, and looked heavenward upon the stars he would have seen. She knew, deep down, she was exactly where she was supposed to be.

"Christmas will find the survivors still on deck," she told the reporter in 1913, "and Chicago will have her Christmas trees as long as the Schuenemanns last." In her hands, Captain Herman's memory was in safe keeping.

True to her word, the captain's bride never missed a Christmas, and she never remarried. She and her three daughters, none of them among the weak of heart, gathered their strength and carried on. Oldest daughter, Elsie, was quoted as saying: "One never knows what one can do until they have to." And she was right.

"As you pass down Clark Street and near the bridge," wrote Barbara Schuenemann's pastor in December of 1932, "you will find a great array of Christmas trees and be greeted with the cordial smile of a dear old mother. She is again busy at her same loving duty, feeling like a newborn child, full of enthusiasm and joy. She is here to help bring joy this year like never before. You all know her. It is

Elsie Schuenemann aboard the ship she sailed in with her mother,
Chicago Daily News, December 6, 1915

good Mother Schuenemann. The *Chicago Tribune* never fails to pay her a tribute of respect and admiration. Her Christmas trees, which she herself sought for in the northwoods of Michigan will adorn the Christian homes of many Chicago citizens this year. Always, there is a desire for green trees when the long night of winter is upon us." The pastor's words became a tribute to Barbara's last Christmas, and a final farewell, after she passed away.

Barbara Schuenemann's death notice, published in June of 1933, memorialized her by saying she was a "remarkable woman whom the people of Chicago loved because of her devotion to the children at Christmastime," and her obituary read, in part: "Mother Schuenemann was known and loved by thousands, and hundreds of thousands, throughout our great metropolis." She was a hearty soul who stayed the course.

The Schuenemann family had served the citizens of Chicago long and well over approximately fifty dedicated years, and they left their impress upon the city. Their legacy lived on for many reasons, not the least of which is that the story exemplifies the best of humanity. Within, we find courage, determination, devotion, generosity, and faith, especially in the heart of the captain.

He knew that somewhere out there heaven lay for the horizon had shown him it was so through the one sight he loved more than any other when he was out to sea. This hope of life eternal, of life evermore, guided him. It was his soul's compass, its beacon, its north star.

"I'll be home soon," he told his dear Barbara when they waved goodbye to one another for the last time.

And so he was. It just hadn't been clear to which home he would be returning that day. It would be the eternal one that unfolded itself around him in those moments when his ship went down and his soul went up, and he was carried by his hope to A Place More Beautiful.

"Yuletide Cargo," painting by Eric Forsberg

Here, beyond the horizon, from the ship of his soul, the captain sails through the unseen passageways of eternity and looks upon forever, and ever, and ever.

Sail on, Captain, sail on.

AFTERWARD

"The influence of each human being on others in this life is a kind of immortality."

President John Quincy Adams

When the tragic news of the Christmas Tree Ship's sinking spread, many believed the legacy of the vessel had come to an end. Little did they know, however, that everything Captain Schuenemann believed in would be alive on shore a hundred years later.

The captain's memory could have melted away like a snowman, but it didn't. He and his ship continue to be remembered by auxiliary members of the Great Lakes Coast Guard who are sustaining a living memorial to the story.

More than a decade has passed since volunteers of the organization resurrected the spirit of the original vessel by giving away thousands of Christmas trees to disadvantaged families in honor of the captain.

The annual event, held at Navy Pier Chicago, was initially triggered by a Coast Guard member who heard about the legendary ship and asked a simple question: "Wouldn't it be great to have a Christmas Tree Ship again?" His vision soon became reality.

More than fifty organizations have shouldered up to the Great Lakes Coast Guard's efforts over the years, including members from the maritime community, churches, and charitable organizations. Every penny donated to the non-profit fund is used for the purchase of trees which are then given away to the less fortunate. The evergreens are chopped and harvested in the great wooded north of Michigan, the same place Captain Schuenemann would have gathered them.

Through the tireless dedication of these volunteers, Captain Schuenemann lives on as an example of how one life can inspire the lives of countless others.

The greatness of the Schuenemann story, indeed of every story, is not how it ends, but how it begins; not how it begins at the beginning, but rather how it begins anew in each heart after the story has ended, or so it may seem.

Volunteer Lynn Koepke recalled a little boy who received a Christmas tree at one of the special Coast Guard ceremonies he attended with his mom and dad. She remembered the child holding onto the tree which was gifted to him, standing as close as possible to it. "He was so excited about that Christmas tree," she said, "and when the volunteers took it from him, to tie it up so it could make the journey home, he burst into tears because he thought they were taking away his tree." After he was reassured that it was only being tied with rope so it could be delivered to his house, his big smile returned.

Another little girl who received a tree thanked the volunteer and added: "I've never had a Christmas tree before." The child's mother, standing beside her, responded: "Neither have I."

Captain Schuenmann, long ago, said he shipped his trees every year because of the joy he found in the eyes of children who came aboard his ship to find the perfect tree for Christmas.

Schuenemann was a man who touched the lives of people he would never know, and the volunteers of Chicago's "new" Christmas Ship are doing the same. They are investing themselves each Christmas in a charitable gift of time to others as they dispel some of the darkness of this "weary world." Theirs is the satisfaction of knowing that a child will awaken on Christmas morning to a tree where no tree would have stood had it not been for the kindness of a stranger. And somewhere, a lifetime from today, these under-privileged recipients may find themselves sharing stories with their children and grandchildren about paste ornaments and tin-foil stars that once decorated a Christmas tree they received as a youngster from a Christmas Ship volunteer who chose to memorialize Captain Santa, a man whose last voyage was not to the bottom of the lake, but into the pages of history.

Every time the captain's memory is recalled, he lives on in the breaths that speak his name, and thus, in the end, it is life, not death, that had the final word on Captain Schuenemann.

"You have not lived a perfect day, even though you have earned your money, unless you have done something for someone who will never be able to repay you."

Ruth Smeltzer

"Whenever I hear anyone arguing for slavery, I feel a strong impulse to see it tried on him personally."

Abraham Lincoln

"Those who deny freedom to others deserve it not for themselves."

Abraham Lincoln

A GIFT FOR PRESIDENT LINCOLN

One of history's most unusual Christmas presents—an entire city—was gifted during the last Christmas of the Civil War in the year 1864 when America was yet a splintered land.

The recipient was President Abraham Lincoln, a man fiercely opposed to slavery, and the giver was Major-General William Tecumseh Sherman.

General Sherman captured Savannah, Georgia, a city known for its slave trade, in December and telegraphed the victorious news to the White House. The communication, dated December 22, arrived on the President's desk on Christmas Eve. It read:

To His Excellency President Lincoln, Washington, D.C.:

I beg to present you as a Christmas gift the city of Savannah, with one hundred and fifty heavy guns and plenty of ammunition, also about twenty-five thousand bales of cotton.

> *W.T. Sherman, Major-General*

President Lincoln's response followed two days later:

My Dear General Sherman,

Many, many thanks for your Christmas gift—the capture of Savannah. When you were about to leave Atlanta for the Atlantic coast, I was anxious, if not fearful; but feeling that you were the better judge, and remembering that "nothing risked nothing gained," I did not interfere. Now, the undertaking being a success, the honor is all yours…

> *Yours very truly,*
> *A. Lincoln*

The Civil War divided America's warring sides into "North" and "South," "blue coats" and "gray coats," "Yankees" and "Johnnies." While Southerners were singing "Dixie," the opposing Northerners were voicing "Yankee Doodle" during a time when our nation was severed on every level and cohesion hung in the balance. Neighbor fought neighbor, brother fought brother, and fathers stood against their own sons when anger was churned up.

By the end of 1864, the country was exhausted of battle—and so were the dispirited soldiers who continued to load cannonballs and gunpowder into horse-drawn wagons. Uniformed troops turned their eyes homeward where their vacated chairs and families were waiting for them.

> Many are the hearts that are weary tonight,
> waiting for the war to cease;
> Many are the hearts looking for the right
> to see the dawn of peace.
>
> Walter Kittredge, 1863

General Sherman, with a steeled resolve, made the pivotal decision to purposely march through the heart of the South at this point and break the will of its people to fight on. It was his view that the conflict would come to a quicker closure, and the country could be seamed, if Southerners faced their inferiority and witnessed war—in totality—on their doorstep.

Atlanta had been captured in September by General Sherman and the assaulted city was torched in November after citizens were ordered to evacuate. Flames spread ruinously and smoke dominated the skyline. Sherman and his men then turned from the scorched earth of Atlanta, in shambles, and swept eastward toward the water's edge. Under the general's able leadership, troops were being strategically—and secretly—maneuvered toward the Atlantic Ocean, but the soldiers had no idea where their boots were marching.

Telegraph lines were cut and railroad tracks were lifted out of place to prevent the release of pertinent information as the army advanced.

A newspaper headline in the *Chicago Tribune* on November 19 asked: "Where is Sherman?" The next day, the *New York Tribune* inked their paper with a similar question: "Where has Sherman Gone?"

Puzzled editors speculated on General Sherman's lengthy

Frank Leslie's Illustrated Newspaper cartoon
"Santa Claus Sherman Putting Savannah into Uncle Sam's Stocking"

absence and his unknown whereabouts. Some wondered if he was "retreating—simply retreating," but the exact opposite was true. Sherman's troops—numbering in the tens of thousands—were on Georgia soil and were "inundating the land like Noah's flood" in a movement forward, with an arrow-straight intent on conquering Savannah. Along the way, attacks continued to be launched.

As troops closed in on Savannah, provisions ran perilously low and the half-starved soldiers were left to survive on minimal rations washed down with swamp water from marshes surrounding the city.

Mandatory orders had been issued for all mail to be held during the arduous march. No correspondence could be sent or received for over a month, and when the backlogged letters—fifteen tons!— were finally delivered to military personnel when they arrived on Savannah's outskirts, one of the serving soldiers acknowledged that he felt "like Rip Van Winkle."

Colonel Absalom H. Markland, who oversaw the mail shipment, introduced himself to Sherman. "I've brought you a message from the President," he began. "He asked me to take you by the hand wherever I met you and say, 'God bless you and the army.' He has been praying for you."

Savannah submitted to Sherman's victorious army in a "bloodless" battle. Confederate troops who defended the city had evacuated during the night in a panicked retreat over a temporary bridge they had constructed. Civilians were left behind. Those who fled were fearful that the charred ruins of Atlanta were a prelude to what could be expected in Savannah, but the city escaped this fate.

A "constant stream" of freed slaves—"old and young, men, women, and children"—extended their gratitude to General Sherman. Henry Hitchcock, who served alongside the general, wrote home to his wife, Mary, and told her how the delivered slaves were "anxious to pay their respects, and to see the man they had heard so much of, and whom—as more than one told him—God had sent as an answer to their prayers. Frequently, they came in a dozen or twenty at a time, to his room upstairs where he usually sits…He has always shown them in at once, stopping a dispatch or letter or conversation to greet them in his offhand, though not undignified, way: 'Well, boys, come to see Mr. Sherman, have you? Well, I'm Mr. Sherman. Good to see you!' He shook hands with them all…Almost all of them who talked spoke of our success and their deliverance with an apparent religious feeling—'Been prayin' for you a long time, sir, prayin' day and night for you, and bless God, you is come.'"

Christmas and General Sherman both arrived in the spared city in 1864 as soldiers tied twigs to the heads of livestock, turning mules into reindeer.

Sherman then gave the order to destroy all of the slave-trade platforms in the city. Former slaves who had been sold like cattle, and who knew what it felt like to stand on top of the auction blocks wearing chains and bruises and scars, watched as the wooden structures were axed into firewood.

Their gift that Christmas was freedom.

PUBLIC SALE OF NEGROES.—Under the authority of a decree of the Circuit Court of Albemarle county, pronouced in the case of Michie's administrator and others, on the 30th day of October, 1855, I will offer for sale, at public auction, on MONDAY, the 5th day of May next, being Albemarle Court day, if a suitable day, if not, on the next suitable day thereafter, at the Court House of Albemarle county, *Five Negroes*, of whom the late David Tichis died possessed, consisting of a Negro Woman, twenty years of age and child two years old, a woman fifty-five years old, a negro man twenty-five years old, who has been working at the slating business, and a negro man twenty-two years old, a blacksmith.— The above lot of negroes is equal to any that has ever been offered in this market.

TERMS OF SALE—Five months credit, negotiable notes with approved endorsers, with the interest added.

ap24—ctds   GEO. DARR, Commissioner.

A Newborn Life
Was in the Manger

"And it came to pass in those days, that there went out a decree from Caesar Augustus that all the world should be taxed. And this taxing was first made when Cyrenius was governor of Syria. And all went to be taxed, every one into his own city. And Joseph also went up from Galilee, out of the city of Nazareth, into Judea, unto the city of David, which is called Bethlehem, because he was of the house and lineage of David, to be taxed with Mary, his espoused wife, being great with child.

"And so it was that while they were there, the days were accomplished that she should be delivered. And she brought forth her firstborn son, and wrapped him in swaddling clothes, and laid him in a manger because there was no room for them in the inn.

"And there were in the same country shepherds abiding in the field, keeping watch over their flock by night. And, lo, the angel of the Lord came upon them, and the glory of the Lord shone round about them, and they were so afraid. And the angel said unto them, 'Fear not! For, behold, I bring you good tidings of great joy which shall be to all people. For unto you is born this day in the city of David a savior, which is Christ the Lord. And this shall be a sign unto you: You shall find the babe wrapped in swaddling clothes, lying in a manger.'

"And suddenly there was with the angel a multitude of the heavenly host praising God, and saying, 'Glory to God in the highest, and on earth peace, goodwill toward men.'

"And it came to pass, as the angels were gone away from them into heaven, the shepherds said one to another, 'Let us now go unto Bethlehem, and see this thing which has come to pass, which the Lord hath made known unto us.'"

Gospel of Luke 2:1-15

It was the first time in as long as anyone could remember that a baby, a real live baby, was asleep in the manger at the old convent.

"Never before," said the sisters who lived there, and their collective memory was nothing short of remarkable.

Many of them—175 total at the time—had spent much of their lives on the hilltop overlooking a small town surrounded by fields and farms. A view of a waterway was just outside their windows where a mill had once operated at the same time the original nuns arrived in 1874 to settle down and call this place home. Surely someone would have remembered if it had happened before, but they didn't, because it hadn't.

And so they came, these sisters, down to the manger at Christmas where a newborn life waited in their midst. They came in their wheelchairs, and they came with their canes, and this was no small feat because these sisters were no stranger to age. They were eighty-years-old, and ninety, and even a hundred. For some, it was a struggle to come forth, and for others it was more than a struggle. Yet these frail ones came. Why? For many, there was only one answer: to see the child. They wished to look upon the miracle called life.

In a scene depicting the silent night, the holy night, a newly-born babe, so fragile and frail, like them, slept in heavenly peace in his mother's arms. The baby was held close to her heart where the prayer for his life had been born long before he had. This woman had waited a very long time for a child. She was nearly forty-years-old, almost beyond child-bearing age, as she waited on. Time slipped, as time does, but her prayer was finally answered.

And then she came to the manger, rejoicing, where she sat down in a worn blue bathrobe, along with a sheet draped around her head and shoulders, to play Mary, mother of Christ. It was her way of thanking God. In this place, she would honor the gift of life—the life of God's Son, and the life of her own.

Her little baby boy was not quite four weeks old. He was just an itty bitty fellow who was born almost a month ahead of schedule. He was supposed to have arrived near Christmastime, but his mother headed to the hospital, instead, during the evening of Thanksgiving Day. It couldn't have been more perfect because her heart was full of gratefulness.

The child, although born prematurely, was also perfect, and the sisters would soon find this out for themselves because they had come not only to see him, but to hold him as well.

A line formed so that all could have a turn. The line stalled only once when one of the nuns was taking longer than the others thought she perhaps should. A nurse standing nearby tried to help.

"Do you see the others waiting?" she asked, addressing the sister. "Wouldn't you like to share the baby?"

The sister's response to the nurse was a simple one. She answered, "No." Those who heard her speak the solitary word couldn't help but smile at the very honest answer. She had spoken the truth.

The baby was passed on eventually, and continued to be passed on, until he was cradled in the arms of a nun who was intent on counting the child's fingers and toes. In order to do this, the elder sister needed to ask the mother to please remove the booties, which she did. You could tell by the look on the other sisters' faces as they watched their friend hold the baby's little hands and feet, and then each arm and leg, that something important was happening. No one said a word, and I wondered about the meaning of the silence.

The elderly nun finally lifted her head and sat still, very still, with the tiny child's arms reaching upward to wrap around her body. Then they held one another, these two, one life soon returning to the heart of God and the other life having just arrived. It was a beautiful sight, and sight in those moments was not to be taken for granted for the sister who had just lifted her head was blind. Her eyes had gone to sleep before she had.

What did she see, this blind one, who stood on the doorstep of eternity as she looked upon the child with her hands instead of her eyes? What thoughts filled her mind?

Perhaps I should have asked, and I would have, had it not been too hard to speak with the lump that filled my throat.

And so I have done some thinking on my own over the years and I wonder if the sister may have thought this: Life is precious. To look upon it in whatever way we can is equally precious. To live and breathe, to love and laugh, to pray and ponder the miracles that fill our moments, if only we will recognize them, is precious.

Could it be this? I wonder.

Bibliography

Chapter 1: World War I Christmas Miracle

Brown, Malcolm and Seaton, Shirley; *Christmas Truce: The Western Front, December 1914*; 1984, Pan Macmillan Ltd., London, England.

Brown, Malcolm; *Meetings in No Man's Land: Christmas 1914 and Fraternization in the Great War*; 2007, Constable & Robinson Ltd., London, England.

Cleaver, Alan and Park, Lesley; *Not a Shot was Fired: Letters from the Christmas Truce 1914*; 2008, published by authors.

Hamilton, Andrew and Reed, Alan; *Meet at Dawn, Unarmed: Captain Robert Hamilton's Account of Trench Warfare and the Christmas Truce in 1914*; 2009, Dene House Publishing, Warwick, England.

Intellectual Reserve, Inc.; *Silent Night, Holy Night: The Story of the Christmas Truce*; 2003, Shadow Mountain, Salt Lake City, UT.

McCutcheon, John; *Christmas in the Trenches*; 2006, Peachtree Publishers, Atlanta, GA.

Murphy, Jim; *Truce*; 2009, Scholastic Press, New York, NY.

Wakefield, Alan; *Christmas in the Trenches*; 2006, Sutton Publishing Ltd., Gloucestershire, England.

Weintraub, Stanley; *Silent Night: The Story of the World War I Christmas Truce*; 2001, Penguin Putnam, New York, NY.

Chapter 2: *A Christmas Carol*

Bowler, Gerry; *The World Encyclopedia of Christmas*; 2000, McClelland & Stewart Ltd., Toronto, Ontario.

Davis, Paul; *The Lives & Times of Ebenezer Scrooge*; 1990, Yale University Press, London, England.

Dickens, Charles; *A Christmas Carol: A Facsimile of the Original Manuscript in The Pierpont Morgan Library with the Illustrations of John Leech and the Text from the First Edition*; 1967, Dover Publications, New York, NY.

Guida, Fred; *A Christmas Carol and its Adaptations: Dickens's Story on Screen and Television*; 2000, McFarland & Company, Inc., Jefferson, NC.

Hearn, Michael Patrick; *The Annotated Christmas Carol*; 2004, W.W. Norton & Company, New York, NY.

Nissenbaum, Stephen; *The Battle for Christmas: A Cultural History of America's Most Cherished Holiday*; 1996, Alfred A. Knopf, Inc., New York, NY.

Restad, Penne; *Christmas in America: A History*; 1995, Oxford University Press, New York, NY.

Sibley, Brian; *A Christmas Carol: The Unsung Story*; 1994, Lion Publishing, Oxford, England.

Standiford, Les; *The Man Who Invented Christmas: How Charles Dickens's A Christmas Carol*

Rescued His Career and Revived our Holiday Spirit; 2008, Crown Publishing Group, New York, NY.

Tabori, Lena; *The Little Big Book of Christmas*; 1999, William Morrow and Company, Inc., New York, NY.

Time-Life Books; *The Time-Life Book of Christmas*; 1987, Alexandria, VA.

Chapter 3: The "Thank You Tree"

Beed, Blair; *1917 Halifax Explosion and American Response*; 1999, Dtours Visitors and Convention Service, Halifax, Nova Scotia.

Bell, Lt. Col. F. McKelvey; *A Romance of the Halifax Disaster*; 1918, The Royal Print & Litho Limited, Halifax, Nova Scotia.

Bird, Michael; *The Town that Died: A Chronicle of the Halifax Disaster*; 1962, McGraw-Hill Ryerson Limited, London, England.

Flemming, David; *Explosion in Halifax Harbour: The Illustrated Account of a Disaster that Shook the World*; 2004, Formac Publishing Company Ltd., Halifax, Nova Scotia.

Griffith, John; *The Halifax Explosion and the Royal Canadian Navy: Inquiry and Intrigue*; 2002, UBC Press, Vancouver, British Columbia.

Kitz, Janet; *Shattered City: The Halifax Explosion and the Road to Recovery*; 1989, Nimbus Publishing, Halifax, Nova Scotia.

MacDonald, Laura; *Curse of the Narrows*; 2005, Walker Publishing Company, Inc., New York, NY.

MacLennan, Hugh; *Barometer Rising*; 1941, McClelland & Steward Ltd., Toronto, Ontario.

MacNeil, Robert; *Burden of Desire*; 1992, Doubleday, New York, NY.

Mahar, James; *Too Many to Mourn: One Family's Tragedy in the Halifax Explosion*; 1998, Nimbus Publishing, Halifax, Nova Scotia.

Metson, Graham; *The Halifax Explosion, December 6, 1917*; 1979, McGraw-Hill Ryerson, Whitby, Ontario.

Monnon, Mary Ann; *Miracles and Mysteries: The Halifax Explosion December 6, 1917*; 1977, Nimbus Publishing, Halifax, Nova Scotia.

Robinson, Ernest Fraser; *The Halifax Disaster, December 6, 1917*; 1987, Vanwell Publishing Ltd., St. Catharine, Ontario.

Sutow, M. Pauline Murphy; *Worse Than War: The Halifax Explosion*; 1992, Four East Publications, Tantallon, Nova Scotia.

Tattrie, Jon; *Black Snow: A Story of Love and Destruction*; 2009, Pottersfield Press, East Lawrencetown, Nova Scotia.

Chapter 4: Saint Nicholas's Golden Gift

Bennett, William; *The True Saint Nicholas: Why He Matters to Christmas*; 2009, Simon & Schuster, New York, NY.

Cann, D.L.; *Saint Nicholas, Bishop of Myra: The Life and Times of the Original Father Christmas*;

2002, Novalis, St. Paul University, Ottawa, Canada.

Carus, Louise; *The Real St. Nicholas: Tales of Generosity and Hope from Around the World*; 2002, Quest Books, Wheaton, IL.

Chris, Teresa; *The Story of Santa Claus: A Delightfully Illustrated History of Everyone's Favorite Saint*; 1992, Chartwell Books, Inc., Edison, NJ.

Crichton, Robin; *Who is Santa Claus? The True Story Behind a Living Legend*; 1987, Canongate Publishing, Edinburgh, Scotland.

Demi; *The Legend of Saint Nicholas*; 2003, Margaret K. McElderry Books, New York, NY.

Ebon, Martin; *Saint Nicholas Life and Legend: The Fascinating Illustrated Story of How the Revered Bishop Nicholas of Myra Evolved into Jolly Old Santa Claus*; 1975, Harper & Row, New York, NY.

Giblin, James Cross; *The Truth About Santa Claus*; 1985, Thomas Y. Crowell, New York, NY.

Jones, Charles; *St. Nicholas of Myra, Bari and Manhattan: Biography of a Legend*; 1978, University of Chicago Press, Chicago, IL.

Jones, E. Willis; *The Santa Claus Book*; 1976, Walker and Company, New York, NY.

Rosenthal, Jim and Wheeler, Joe; *St. Nicholas: A Closer Look at Christmas*; 2005, Thomas Nelson, Inc., Nashville, TN.

Seal, Jeremy; *Nicholas: The Epic Journey from Saint to Santa Claus*; 2005, Bloomsbury Publishing, New York, NY.

Stiegemeyer, Julie; *Saint Nicholas: The Real Story of the Christmas Legend*; 2003, Concordia Publishing House, St. Louis, MO.

Tompert, Ann; *Saint Nicholas*; 2000, Boyds Mills Press, Honesdale, PA.

Yzermans, Vincent; *Wonderworker: The True Story of How St. Nicholas Became Santa Claus*; 1994, ACTA Publications, Chicago, IL.

Chapter 5: A Great Depression Good Samaritan

Gup, Ted; *A Secret Gift: How One Man's Kindness—and a Trove of Letters—Revealed the Hidden History of the Great Depression*; 2010, Penguin Group, New York, NY.

Chapter 6: Good King Wenceslas

Charles IV, Holy Roman Emperor of Luxemburg, King of Bohemia, edited by Nagy, Balazs and Schaer, Frank; *Autobiography of Emperor Charles IV and His Legend of St. Wenceslas* (Medieval Text); 2001, Central European University Press, Budapest, Hungary. (Includes the first English translation of the Legend of Saint Wenceslas by Charles IV. Contains both the Latin narrative sources and a complete English-language translation. It is one of the few autobiographies to have survived from the Middle Ages, written by one of the most influential rulers of the fourteenth century.)

Hucek, Miroslav; *The Castle of Prague and Its Treasures*; 1994, The Vendome Press, New York, NY.

Hutsky, Matthias with translation by Heller, Martin; *Life and Martyrdom of St. Wenceslas,*

Prince of Bohemia, in Historic Pictures—Prague 1585; 1997, Opus Publishing, London, England. (This is a facsimile of a 16th-century manuscript.)

Luckhardt, Mildred Corell; *Good King Wenceslas*; 1964, Abingdon Press, Nashville, TN.

Maiden, Cecil; *A Song for Young King Wenceslas*; 1969, Addison-Wesley Publishing Company, Inc., Reading, MA.

Rejzl, Jan; *Good King Wenceslas: The Real Story*; 1995, 1st Choice Publishing Limited, Norwich, Great Britain.

Chapter 7: "'Twas the Night Before Christmas"

"Coronet" magazine, December 1945, Volume 19, Number 2; Pages 26-31: "A Father's Gift to All Children."

Del Re, Gerard and Patricia; *The Story of "'Twas the Night Before Christmas:" The Life and Times of Clement Clarke Moore and His Best-Loved Poem of Yuletide*; 1991, Wynwood Press, Grand Rapids, MI.

Haight, Anne Lyon; Collection at the Hunt Library, Carnegie Mellon University, Pittsburgh, PA; Donated in 1982. The collection, with items numbering in the hundreds, contains over 300 editions of the poem in book form. All known publications of the poem in its first fifty years of existence are included in original form with the exception of only its very first publication in the *Troy Sentinel* newspaper in 1823.

Hall, Gladys; *All About "The Night Before Christmas;"* 1918, Cupples & Leon Company, New York, NY.

Hosking, Arthur; *"The Night Before Christmas:" The True Story of "A Visit from St. Nicholas" with A Life of the Author Clement C. Moore*; 1934, Dodd, Mead and Company, New York, NY.

Irving, Washington; *Old Christmas*; 1892, Macmillan and Company, London, England.

Krehbiel Company; *An Historical Sketch of the Origin and Conception of the Poem "A Visit from St. Nicholas;"* 1930, The C. J. Krehbiel Company, Cincinnati, OH.

"Life" magazine; *"A Visit from St. Nicholas;"* Volume 31, Number 24, December 10, 1951, Pages 96-100; Includes the complete illuminations of Mary Ogden.

Marshall, Nancy; *"The Night Before Christmas:" A Descriptive Bibliography of Clement Clarke Moore's Immortal Poem with Editions from 1823 through 2000*; 2002, Oak Knoll Press, New Castle, Delaware.

Marshall, Nancy; Collection at the Earl Gregg Swem Library, The College of William and Mary, Williamsburg, VA; Donated in 2005. The collection, consisting of over 1,000 items pertaining to Clement C. Moore and his poem, is the largest collection previously held in private hands.

Moore, James; *Reverend John Moore of Newtown, Long Island, and Some of His Descendants*; 1903, Lafayette College, Easton, PA. (Includes a portrait of Moore, an engraving of his home in Chelsea, a reproduction of a holograph copy of the poem, and an article about the poet explaining the genealogy of his immediate family, including grandparents, parents, wife, children, and descendants.)

Moulton, Mark Kimball; *The Visit: The Delightful History and Origin of "The Night Before*

Christmas" as Recalled by Florence Dinghy Sharp, Storyteller and Great-Great Granddaughter of the Author, Clement Clarke Moore; 2001, Lang Books, Delafield, WI.

Ogden, David, great-great-great grandson of Clement C. Moore; *"A Visit from St. Nicholas" by Clement C. Moore with Illuminations by Mary C. Ogden, Daughter of Clement C. Moore*; 1995, International Resourcing Services, Inc., Northbrook, IL.

Patterson, Samuel; *Old Chelsea and St. Peter's Church*; 1935, The Friebele Press, New York, NY.

Patterson, Samuel; *The Poet of Christmas Eve: A Life of Clement Clarke Moore, 1779-1863, Author of "A Visit from St. Nicholas;"* 1956, Morehouse-Gorham Co., New York, NY.

Pelletreau, William; *"The Night Before Christmas:" The Poem and Its History*; 1897, G. W. Dillingham Company, New York, NY.

Sherman, Mary Moore; *Recollections of Clement C. Moore by His Granddaughter*; 1906, Knickerbocker Press, New York, NY.

Turner, Thyra; *Christmas House: The Story of "A Visit from St. Nicholas;"* 1943, Charles Scribner's Sons, New York, NY.

Chapter 8: The Christmas Tree Ship

Pennington, Rochelle; *The Historic Christmas Tree Ship: A True Story of Faith, Hope, and Love*; 2004, Pathways Press, West Bend, WI.

Chapter 9: A Gift for President Lincoln

Bailey, Anne; *War and Ruin: William T. Sherman and the Savannah Campaign*; 2003, Scholarly Resources, Inc., Wilmington, DE.

Daiss, Timothy; *Rebels, Saints, Sinners: Savannah's Rich History and Colorful Personalities*; 2002, Pelican Publishing Company, Gretna, LA.

Hines, Barbara and Russell, Preston; *Savannah: A History of her People Since 1733*; 1992, Frederic C. Beil, Savannah, GA.

Jakes, John; *Savannah: Or a Gift for Mr. Lincoln*; 2004, Penguin Group, New York, NY.

Jones, Jacqueline; *Saving Savannah: The City and the Civil War*; 2008, Alfred A. Knopf, New York, NY.

Lawrence, Alexander; *A Present for Mr. Lincoln: The Story of Savannah from Secession to Sherman*; 1997, The Oglethorpe Press, Inc., Savannah, GA.

McIvor, James; *God Rest Ye Merry, Soldiers: A True Civil War Christmas Story*; 2006, Penguin Group, New York, NY.

Weintraub, Stanley; *General Sherman's Christmas, Savannah, 1864*; 2009, HarperCollins Publishers, New York, NY.